THE CONTENT REVOLUTION

Published by
LID Publishing Ltd
Garden Studios, 71-75 Shelton Street
Covent Garden, London WC2H 9JQ

31 West 34th Street, Suite 7004,
New York, NY 10001, US

info@lidpublishing.com
www.lidpublishing.com

A member of:

www.businesspublishersroundtable.com

Printed in Great Britain by TJ International
ISBN: 978-1-907794-87-2

Cover & page design: Laura Hawkins

THE CONTENT REVOLUTION

Communicate what you stand for
by telling a better story

MARK MASTERS

LONDON MONTERREY
MADRID SHANGHAI
MEXICO CITY BOGOTA
NEW YORK BUENOS AIRES
BARCELONA SAN FRANCISCO

CONTENTS

This book is dedicated to Kate.
Who taught me to go hard or go home.
Without her, this story would not have happened.

FOREWORD
BY ROBERT ROSE

ARE YOU A REVOLUTIONARY OR REFUGEE?

Marketing has lost its way.

Sixty years ago, famed author and business management consultant Peter Drucker said that the '*purpose of a business is to create a customer. The business enterprise has two – and only two – basic functions; marketing and innovation.*' In its time, it was true. During the 1960s, the idea of a 'brand manager' was the equivalent of what we look at today as a 'social media manager'; an extraordinarily innovative and fashionable role that was considered (as some marketing textbooks claimed) the 'backbone of true marketing'. It would be a mere 30 years later that the idea of marketing and the 'brand manager' would be called 'ill suited for today's environment'. And, where the role of marketing would be that which '*cannot dominate, but rather must share power with other functions to ensure competitive advantage*'.

The past 15 years have seen consumer behaviour change fundamentally. The way customers become aware, browse, investigate, purchase, use, complain, and/or become loyal to the way a brand delivers its product or service has changed. However, the business processes to facilitate this awareness, shopping, differentiation, use, and service have not. Marketing departments in today's business serve mostly a subservient, on-demand function; producing ever-more sales sheets, PDFs, brochures, and copy for an ever-hungry business that views it as the department that 'makes things pretty'.

This must stop, or the business will fail. Business as usual just is not possible any longer.

Put simply: the time is ripe for marketers to reclaim both values of marketing and innovation as the unique and distinguishing function of the business. But the opportunity will pass, and the revolution may quiet. We have a choice. We can be revolutionary, or refugees.

WELCOME TO THE EVOLUTION

It seems clear now that the evolution of marketing more broadly will move beyond the goal of simply 'creating a customer' (as Drucker said). In fact, creating a customer is simply table stakes for most marketing organizations. The new objective for marketing will be to *evolve customers,* from unaware all the way to brand-subscribing customer advocates. Content-driven experiences will be the natural selection process that moves that customer through that evolution.

That's the part that has changed. Whether it's due to the digital disruption and ease by which we now publish and distribute content and experiences to aggregate our own audiences, or just the natural evolution of marketing itself does not matter as much as the ultimate outcome. We've absolutely seen evidence of this in all the research, advisory clients, and our own executive forum. Companies that have successfully created a process, through which to deliver valuable content-driven experiences worry less about the specific structure of the group and where it sits in the company hierarchy; they focus on content itself as a recognized, valuable, and discrete function in the business.

And this is where we come to the extraordinary book you are about to read. What Mark has been able to do is construct a powerful story, in and of itself, and weave in an extraordinary argument that will change beliefs. It is a book of transformation; of how marketing departments need to disrupt themselves and move from a focused strategy of self-promotion and interruption-based tactics, into a mindset built to create credible, emotional, influential, trustworthy, and (most of all) valuable content-driven experiences.

It's a hero's journey, and one that should not be taken lightly. But it will be a bold adventure …

So, if you're ready …

ROBERT ROSE
Chief Strategy Officer, Content Marketing Institute
September 2014

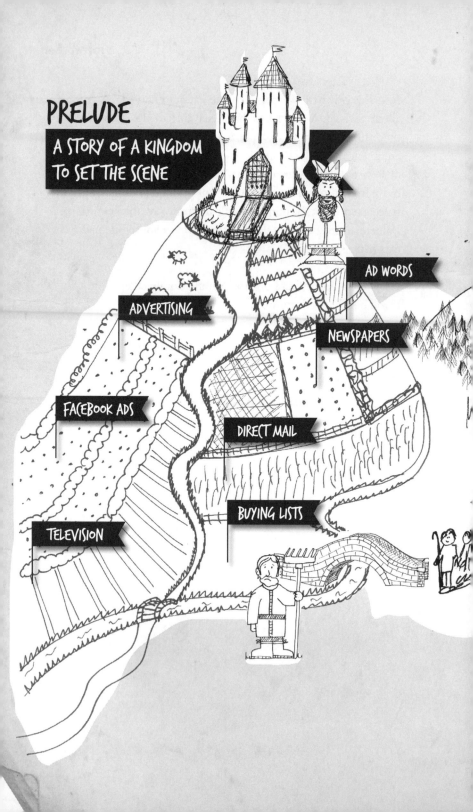

PRELUDE

A STORY OF A KINGDOM
TO SET THE SCENE

AD WORDS

ADVERTISING

NEWSPAPERS

FACEBOOK ADS

DIRECT MAIL

TELEVISION

BUYING LISTS

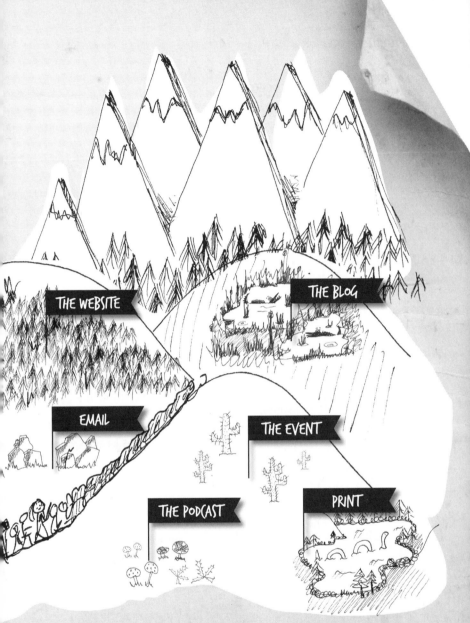

Here is a short story that has relevance to the way business is today. Let's go back to a mythical land that was ruled and governed by a powerful elite.

ONCE UPON A TIME there was a kingdom that was controlled by the powerful. Those who owned the land ruled the land.

THE RULERS had inherited the land from their predecessors and had the power to dictate, direct, and govern. The biggest asset that had accumulated over the years was land; the power to trade and the ability to build a kingdom. The domain, over which they had control, was uncontested and reliant on a way of working that had been in place for many years. The influence and capability to make decisions was well and truly with the rich – the landed gentry.

EVERYONE ELSE underneath the land-owning elite was employed to generate profits and had the responsibility to farm the land. In return for working for the owners, they were paid for their keep but control was well and truly with those who owned the land. The land was allocated and then tended for a return so the farmers could feed their families and enjoy the smaller things in life, but they were limited in the amount of flexibility and autonomy.

They experienced the wish to break away and look at potential future horizons was nothing more than a pipe dream as the cost of implementing this was often imagined to be unsustainable. The landowners controlled the budgets and allocation of spend. The farmers who worked the land within the kingdom were treated as nothing more than cogs in a system that did not care about them (well, apart from the turkey that was provided by the landowners as a Christmas present, a mere gesture of gratitude).

HOW THIS APPLIES TO THE REAL WORLD

The land-owning elite are those companies that have been part of the commercial landscape for many years; some are now becoming lazy in their approach. They believe that their brand and heritage carries enough weight to ensure loyalty. However, times are changing and their complacency is now giving opportunity to others.

People are educated from a young age to follow a hierarchical class system and fit into roles within this – led by occupations. Consequently, within businesses, this hierarchy also exists. Larger companies, notably those with bigger budgets and market share, have inherently owned significant proportions of the marketplace. This system has been generationally accepted as part of the established order. It is possible to move up this hierarchy by fitting in but 'starting at the bottom'. There has been acceptance that larger companies will always be bigger and cannot be challenged with a 'David and Goliath' mentality.

THE OPPORTUNITY THAT AROSE

Outside the immediate kingdom there was land in the far-off distance that was uncharted.

The problem in the more remote regions was that farmers would have to take a different approach to farming the arable land that was in abundance within the controlled areas (but owned by others). The alternative land in the remote regions could be farmed but had deficiencies such as being nutrient poor, a lack of immediate water, or areas that were rocky. While not too much was known about the foreign lands, it was acknowledged that it would be tough and take commitment, dedication, and longevity to convert it into arable land, but it was possible for the land to become a source of abundance if it was farmed well, season after season, year after year. It was acknowledged that the land could become fertile but only through a smarter approach to farming and accepting personal responsibility for future development.

The intrigue and promise was driven by a desire to break free from a rigid regime that had been in place for many years. The new land was not owned by anyone or currently farmed. It was unclaimed, but within touching distance once links were created from the existing land to the new space.

The land in the existing kingdom had been farmed a particular way for decades. The strategies in place had been handed down from generation to generation, but it was becoming clear that the overworked land was not as fertile as it had been. As a result, the traditional techniques of farming no longer produced the same yield; they needed to be adapted to allow for change in the land. However, convention dedicated doing things the way they had always because this had always produced results.

To those who accepted the overworked land was no longer as fertile, the dreams of taking ownership of a new space was to become a commitment to explore further. Through research, belief, and understanding, the tentative steps were made to invest time and energy within the new land.

HOW THIS APPLIES TO THE REAL WORLD
The new land is represented by digital spaces, namely your website, your blog, and your email. Through using more modern techniques to nurture an audience, you are able to build the connection with the consumer to generate profitable action.

The traditional marketing methods such as press advertising, direct marketing, and the disruption and interruption of an audience do not produce results/a yield in this new land. Instead, we need to learn to use newer techniques, which may take longer to deliver a return, but once established can produce more sustainable growth. This initially takes a leap of faith and requires a change in mindset, but the result is that your space is 100% owned by you.

THE COMMITMENT THAT WAS MADE

The first acknowledgment was the requirement to farm in a different way. New irrigation canals and wells were created, new trees were planted, and alternative insulation was developed against the cold and the heat, along with protection against the wind. This had to be learned and implemented to aggregate a fruitful harvest, but it could be achieved. People realized they could build momentum and expertise in new methods and this could, in turn, pave the way for their land to grow and challenge the land-owning aristocracy from the old kingdom. A revolt was quietly happening. They knew that before long they would have the ability to achieve far more than being at the whim of those who had built a rigid structure.

To those who had tried to generate a harvest on a new piece of land, the main drive for change was a future, that was not going to be about power and proclamation, but to be the centre of something that was built with an individual's own hands and belief that a new harvest was possible. Instead of being envied for what they had achieved, people would be respected for what had been built. Rather than being run by generational acceptance of the powerful elite, the movement into new spaces and harvesting new land was built on the quest for learning and collaborating with others. In this new land, farming methods were not kept under lock and key.

As the new land became more fertile, the respect from others increased; they could see that the marketplace was growing. What was gradually becoming evident was a movement from an old system that was based on hierarchy and inheritance to one of a flatter structure. Practices could be implemented at a faster pace and a democracy was built where the focus was more on developing individual relationships and alliances made. The pioneers who farmed the new land were prepared to re-educate themselves in the new practices and had made a decision to change.

The new land that was being farmed was on an equal standing with the longer-established kingdom. For those who were successful, the farming of the new land was more than a discipline: it became a habit. The traits of the farmers represented leadership, respect, trust, and authenticity.

The links to the new land grew gradually over time. What was once an inconsistent path, clearings, trees, and shrubbery, was now becoming littered with accessible road providing easy access and the ability to interact with other regions. What was once an unstable wooden plank over a stretch of water was now a sturdy bridge from one side of the land to the other. The access to the land was becoming more mobile and this contributed to the success of the ongoing farming and growth of the land. Eventually, it was becoming recognized as a more trusted producer than the longer-running kingdom.

The original kingdom had, for many years, become set in its ways and worked to an old system using technology and application that had been part of its culture for many decades. It had neglected to accept the new methods and had not adapted over time.

The new farmers who sourced new land and decided to make a commitment to learn, had gradually positioned themselves as the authority in a new land. It was recognized that they did not have to be big to be successful; they had to be significant in what they did. The new ways of working relied on understanding new traits and being prepared for the long term. Clinging to nostalgia and old ways of working was recognized as a trait from a bygone age and the owners of the old kingdom were welcome to it.

The revolution that started from a change of mindset and a quest to look at new land to farm and grow had now become regarded as the accepted practice, everyday. The farmers who tended to the new land had discovered that they were now "discoverable".

HOW THIS APPLIES TO THE REAL WORLD

By building your own domain, you can generate a conversation and grow an audience that belongs to you alone. This approach is more engaging and more targeted as it is grown organically and is therefore more likely to produce a 'yield' or business growth. You can now be regarded as the authority in your marketplace by delivering a consistent message that meets the needs of your audience.

As businesses, we need to re-educate ourselves to use communication tools in a committed manner that is not reliant on tired marketing methods (interruption, disruption, and self-promotion). We need to become self-sufficient by having an understanding of technology, our marketplace, and the consistent content that we need to deliver. The ability to build a successful brand in today's world is not about creating a fantastic logo and self-promotional print. It is not about being the biggest and having an endless marketing budget, but the ability to present a brand persona to which an audience can relate and of which people want to be part.

INTRODUCTION

Before we get stuck in, this book has nothing to do with social media or a road map to make you the 'go to' expert in your profession. If you want that, then put the book down now and let's agree that we were never meant to be.

However, if you are looking for a way to grow your business, this book will help you understand how nurturing a loyal audience can help you achieve this goal.

This book also identifies the merits of adopting a content marketing approach. Content has now become a vital tool of the buying process. Businesses need to become more useful, interesting, and entertaining to their audiences. They can do this by delivering the right type of information with which others will feel compelled to interact and relate. The stories that a business can tell become a strong form of competitive advantage. When the time comes to buy, the consumer has already made up their mind because they know, like, and trust the company that has embraced a content mindset.

The consumer is now well and truly in control. They are becoming far better informed; they can connect with businesses on a level never known before in the history of mankind. They can jump from desktop to tablet to phone and purchase in different ways. Our challenge is to find the right language to get others to connect and engage with us in a world in which everyone is fighting to be heard.

Many businesses have taken to the podium in recent years as the 'expert', but this is the wrong approach to sell to your audience and promotes disengagement. The world is bulging with people who claim to be the 'font of knowledge'. However, only a handful of people have dedicated themselves to the study, which allows this title. The good news is that you do not need to be an expert to connect with your audience. In fact, what you need to be is fresh, challenging, and provide information that is relevant to your audience's learning and decision-making.

Instead of marketing ourselves as experts, we need to recognize that we are enthusiasts and are still learning the tools of our trade. The benefit of this is that those with an honest voice, who are able to share their experiences, can become a high-demand resource in their own right. Others can learn from the journey they have been on and the decisions they have made. Speaking in a way in which an audience relate and empathize, can position you as a trusted adviser.

Let's take things back to our schooldays. We all cherished picking our team, whether it related to study or sport. The first members we picked for our team were never really those who were the best, but were predominantly with whom we got on and hung around. These were people we cared about and in our immediate circle of trust. The similarity between our youth and adulthood is we will invariably prefer working with those with whom we make a connection.

As businesses, we need to create the whole package that is more than being 'experts' in the aim of standing out from the rest. We need to be creative, confident, have a track record, show humility, and take responsibility for those we serve. We need to solve problems and create better experiences for others. People do not necessarily select the 'expert', but the one to whom they can relate on a personal and emotional level. Rather than brazenly saying that we are the industry 'expert' to which others should flock, we need to be aware of our strengths and weaknesses and tune our energy in to what we stand for and the opinions we have.

I originally thought that to be chosen, we had to be considered the best. This is a continuous journey we are all on and we cannot be afraid of change. Our goal is to explore and share the experiences that make us better people and represent strong business.

Consumers need to make an association with your business, so that you stand out from your competition. But how do you enable this?

This book is broken down into two sections. The first part is what we need to do as businesses to reflect on where we currently are. In the second half, we will look at the opportunities that are available and more affordable than ever before to grow your audience, utilize content, and drive sales in a space of which you have complete control.

CHAPTER 1

Control is now well and truly with the business owner.

Until recently, businesses have been held hostage by the media. The media has controlled dialogue with its audience by setting pricing structures with which companies have had to engage. Your budget gave you rented space, in the form of advertising, to target an audience that belonged to someone else.

Throughout the 20th century and part of the 21st century, businesses have had to rely on others to distribute our messages and collateral. However, the rules have now changed.

Affordable technology is now letting businesses shape what they say and to whom they say it, but more importantly you can become more creative than ever before with less money. The creation of engaging content is changing the landscape for both businesses and individuals looking to build credibility, influence, and trust. The key is the movement from interruption to becoming useful, and the transition from paid-for media advertising to having control of the platforms you use and ownership of what is yours.

It's not only the platforms that represent the opportunity but also the infrastructure that gives us freedom. According to Start-Up Britain, an initiative of the Centre For Entrepreneurs (CFE), 581,173 new businesses were started by British entrepreneurs in

2014 (as of 31st December 2014). This is up from 526, 446 in 2013 and 484,224 in 2012.

The phenomena of more businesses entering our respective marketplaces highlights the new-found freedom and ease of making decisions, discovering new spaces, building new audiences and generating a customer base.

THE DREAMS WE HAD

What was once a vision and a desire to break free from the responsibilities of working for someone else is now a reality. People are looking to control their own journeys by starting their own businesses.

The vision can be realized at a more cost-effective level at which we can build our platform online and offline, have a dialogue with an audience, and stand up and be noticed.

The barriers to launching a business are now fewer than ever before. Although the majority of small and medium businesses account for 99.9% of all private sector businesses in the UK, according to Business Population Estimates (BPE), the majority of businesses think and act similarly. To build a successful business you need to stand out from the crowd.

THE MESSAGE YOU CURATE

In his book *Your Brand, The Next Media Company*, author on social business and content strategy, Michael Brito, describes society as living in a world of 'content surplus and attention deficit'. We can see there are more of us competing for the attention of others; buyers have more choice than they have ever had and can consume information in any format and from a host of channels whenever and wherever suits them.

There may be more than half a million businesses in the UK and the majority may represent a case of 'me-too' personas, but those who choose to stand for something and represent what they believe in, can break free from everyone else and let their ideas spread. Consumption is no longer based on how important the person is or who is distributing the information, but how relevant and useful the idea is.

NOW IS THE BEST TIME TO BE IN BUSINESS TO MAKE AN IMPACT IN THIS NEW DAWN

The old world represented the dictation of a message to an audience and that message was either repeated or moulded into another form to interrupt and disrupt. From press, radio, TV, advertising, and other forms of paid-for media such as direct marketing (DM) to the good old-fashioned route of cold-calling, a product-driven way to converse, interact, and sell was the norm. To the consumer, there were very few sources of information they could access before making a decision. Moving into today's world, IBM's mindboggling statistic that 90% of the data in the world today has been created in the past two years puts everything into perspective. Not only do we have an information overload but also, when information is distributed and managed carefully, ideas can change the world and business owners can become a catalyst for change based on what they care for and stand for.

Content has built momentum on such a scale that it is difficult to ignore. From its role as a Search Engine Optimisation (SEO) tool, to being a marketing mindset, we need to evolve from telling the consumer how good we are to now proving how useful we can be. We now need to aim to become more altruistic by helping others, and being informative and of value, as opposed to stating that you are the best in your industry. What is important to understand is that no matter how considered and meaningful your content is, it does not mean anything if there is no audience willing to hear what you have to say.

AUDIENCE = MARKETPLACE

Having an audience is the biggest factor in helping you to grow your business.

We are all now predisposed to collecting numbers for the sake of collecting numbers in the ongoing pursuit of popularity. Gaining followers, likes, and plus ones is similar to playing a video game simply to gain bragging rights about having more points than anyone else. Being popular is the last thing you should ever want to become. Instead, you want the people who form your audience to be listening to you, actively ready to engage and participate in your conversations. Building an audience that has longevity and staying power is your commitment to being consistent. Collecting numbers has never mattered; what is important is how we connect with others on a personal level. Whether this is via a weekly digest of news from your website or a monthly newsletter, what you have to do is keep to it to earn the attention of others, but also reinvent the channels that have perhaps become neglected (such as your email and your website).

The challenge for businesses is to continually refine and develop audiences through the content programmes that we use and define readers as real people rather than an homogenous mass. You only have to look at your Facebook timeline to see the vast array of paid-for ads, that do not resonate with you.

HUMANIZING A DIGITAL WORLD

One thing that has not changed since the dawn of time, no matter how big the technological advances have been, is the need for businesses and people to build relationships. People do business with those they know, like, and trust. We were all once limited geographically, now we can profit financially, intellectually, and emotionally from the worlds we create.

Although technology can break down barriers and entry to market, one thing will always remain constant and that is who we are as people. The dehumanizing of the way we communicate via templates and automation to connect to others is the equivalent of a warm comfort blanket that shields us from being public and personable.

When businesses look at the role of social media, it does not change the way we interact. It is, in essence, another method of communicating with a long-term goal of generating conversation, building rapport, and interaction. However, it becomes lazy to think that all roads lead to Rome (aka Twitter, Facebook, LinkedIn, and Google+).

Do we really think that the world of social media will help us lead better and more fulfilled lives?

The plethora of platforms show that it is becoming easier to hide behind a faceless product and then dictate a message to an audience. We only have to look as far as the automated LinkedIn invitation email waiting for us in our inboxes with the lack of authenticity and the 'I'd like to connect with you on LinkedIn'. Sending a templated message with a ready-made sign-off lets everyone know that the individuality you once had is now replaced by an automated email in a tone of voice that is not representative of who you are.

Communication has shifted us to a world that is overloaded with connection invitations. The challenge and opportunity for businesses is to find our own voices, become more human, and nurture the flow of interactions with prospective customers and those within our audience who have earned our trust. The social media platforms that are available to us all represent a completely different way of doing business to build relationships and generate conversation; it's just a case of using them in a way that positions you as the leader in your marketplace.

Taking warmth and comfort in connectivity with others but hiding behind a digital persona, is a recipe for merely blending in with the crowd. Look around you at those who are still selling their products by dictating a message: what they should be doing is adding value through sharing information that is relevant to the interests of others. Your ultimate aim is to make the lives of your audience better, easier, and more time-rich. Think of it this way: imagine that you are a librarian and your customer is looking for a book on a particular subject. Rather than expecting your customer to search around a host of aisles, you could provide the information they need a lot quicker as you understand the information available.

The security blanket needs to be kicked off and instead you need to become more present and champion being human again.

The other benefit of a shift to a more content-driven approach is that we own the audience we have built and have a more personal connection with members.

CONTROL WITH THE BUSINESS OWNER

Your website and email address represent what is rightfully yours and it is your duty to own them. Never look to build these on someone else's terms. When you hand over ownership, you lose control. This even applies to another company owning your website and being responsible for its updates (and charging you for it). You will never make your website an evolving process when you have one eye on invoices that are sent to you for changes made.

Anyone who thinks that Facebook and Twitter are spaces owned and controlled by themselves is crazy. You may think that you own your content but someone else can use it whenever and however they want. You only have to read through Twitter's 'worldwide, non-exclusive, royalty-free license, with the right to sublicense' to realize that this is the case. These sites are useful for distributing our message but they come at a cost. Social media platforms are not charities, they are here to utilize the information that we provide. Building your platform in someone else's space is not the way forward for creating an online arena and we forfeit any intellectual property rights we thought we owned.

When you convert followers on your social sites to subscribers to your website, then you will start to reap the rewards.

BECOMING OUR OWN MEDIA COMPANIES

If you are here to embrace change, this is the greatest time to be in business. According to Trevor Young, author of *microDOMINATION*, 'to be able to cost-effectively create your own content at scale; to be able to leverage social media channels to grow your audience and deepen the intensity of connection you have with your constituents, is truly amazing.'

The old way of doing business was limited by cost and this became the biggest stumbling block for businesses to present their image to the world. However, in a new digital age the only thing that can limit you is the failure to generate an idea and see it through. The greatest investment you now require is your time. Technology is allowing us to enter markets a lot more quickly and easily. You now have the ability to create, curate, and self-publish relevant (and entertaining) information, to have a two-way conversation, to nurture new customers and to help build a community of others who stand by what you believe in. You also have the opportunity to reinvent the channels that have become neglected (such as print). We are all effectively media companies and the reward is there for businesses that can tell a compelling story. Tactics that are available on both an online and offline platform are plentiful; let no-one suggest that traditional methods do not have a place anymore. There is a place for all forms of communication as long as the message is interesting to the target audience.

One story that has always stuck with me since my schooldays is the 'ant and the grasshopper':

An ant spent the summer collecting and storing food in preparation for the relentless winter months. Meanwhile, the grasshopper basked in the good weather that the summer months delivered and enjoyed what it provided. When winter came, the ant had worked diligently throughout the previous months to still be able to eat, whereas the grasshopper was left with nothing.

What this story represents in a modern world is not in the moral of 'if you work hard, you can reap the rewards'; it is deeper than that. The grasshopper represents those businesses that have become lazy. We cannot sit back and wait for things to happen. Building growth takes patience and those that focus on the here and now, instead of planning for the future, will end up weakened.

The grasshopper represents a business that is happy to stick with what has been done before and the tried-and-tested routes to market (with the same results). Becoming comfortable in the light of past successes becomes a habit.

The world of the ant represents the new world, where investment in relationships and playing the long game take precedence. Being like the ant means being consistent and continuous in the content you produce, rather than focused on self-promotion.

The ant represents a business that has persistence. These businesses embrace change and adjust to new ways of working, where being human and connecting with others in a more creative way can provide the path for longevity and success.

THE CHANNELS YOU SHOULD USE TO CREATE, CURATE, AND PUBLISH

Creating content is not difficult, but creating quality content that can be heard is. This is good news for those who produce the content that their audience demands. Your job is to curate and publish content that engages them.

Having a website alone is not on its own enough to guarantee an audience: any company can have a website. Instead, we need to learn who our audience is and produce content specifically for them.

Measuring different types of content produced on various platforms can drive success. What is key is the measurement metrics you are aiming to use to determine the merit of each activity. Here are some ways used to assess the quality of the content produced.

Website and blogs – using platforms such as Wordpress can enable those who have subscribed to receive content (hopefully on a regular basis):

- you can link relevant articles on your site to other pages that have similar themes
- other people can comment and interact with the discussion on your site via plug-ins that can be easily installed
- there is proof that you create regular, relevant content
- what you create can be shared on the various social media platforms (Twitter, Facebook, LinkedIn)

Video – YouTube and Vimeo have established themselves as the platforms for presenting video:

- all uploaded content highlights the number of views and comments
- there is the ability to like and share video content on other

platforms and also easy to embed this within your own site

Guides and eBooks have developed in prominence:
- we can measure how many people have downloaded a copy
- we can measure who has shared on the various social media platforms

Webinars and in-person events are regarded by many as the most effective content marketing channels, where each of the following is easily measurable:
- the number of people who signed up is visible
- the number of people who were present at the event
- the number of people who viewed the presentation after the event, online

Businesses should not focus on their own self-promotion, but on having an honest approach that assures they can deliver.

As business owners, we must always look to earn the trust of others to help build profitable action. It's not just a case of adding value but also sticking to the principles that we set out to represent. We all started our businesses with something in which we believed, from making a working process easier to knowing that we were talented in a particular skill set. We need to remember these principals to guide our message of what we stand for.

We can do this by being more realistic and having an honest connection with people, by being transparent, responsive and, above all else, keeping our promises.

Keeping and delivering on your promises lends credibility to your business and what you stand for. This now allows us to move on to the traits we need to have to position ourselves as a credible resource.

CHAPTER 2

From a young age, we were taught that fitting in was good. This stared at school: where we were taught how to conform to rules and how to apply ourselves in a uniform way to achieve success. However, in business the reverse applies.

Is it not time to stand out from the crowd and position yourself as an influencer?

There were 5.2 million private sector businesses in the UK (at the start of 2014), the highest since estimates began in 2000, according to Business Population Estimates (BPE).

The only way to stand out is to become the person (or brand) others want to listen to.

The more you inspire others, the bigger your audience will become. However, to be seen as better than the competition, you need to be seen as *an* authority, *a* leader, and *a* key influencer. This then means that you have access to a marketplace. If there is one common goal for successful business owners to share, it is the building of a brand that becomes integral to a community and, even more importantly, useful.

To be seen as an influencer in your industry, you need to follow these five steps:

- have a mindset of making change by acknowledging the problems you want to solve
- recognize there is an audience which will be receptive to the solution you deliver
- accept there will be others who will never understand (or bother to understand) what you stand for
- use the most appropriate platforms to deliver your message to your audience, in a way they understand and with which they engage
- be consistent and continuous with your message to your audience

However, before you can go ahead and become recognized as a key influencer within your industry, you need to follow the following steps for more definition:

- define who you are
- build a personality
- stand for something
- build your audience/community
- make a connection
- promote
- over-deliver

DEFINE WHO YOU ARE

If you want your business to succeed, help solve problems for others. Is that not the reason you went into business in the first place, to provide a service to which people would flock?

You have to make a decision to not stand in the middle of the road like everyone else. If you stand in that central spot, eventually everyone will go round you (or ignore you) or worse still, hit you head-on. What you have to take on board is the self-belief to provide the right solution for a targeted audience by thinking about the information your customers need. However, to produce content that is useful, you have to address a problem that has not been solved by someone else. It is only by going 'against the grain' that you will begin to position yourself as different from everyone else.

Customers do not want to be sold to; what they want are their hopes, needs, and wants catered for. It is your opportunity to find something that is going to set you apart from the crowd and for your audience to love the way that you do things.

Here are some examples with a different slant on products:

- if you own a restaurant, do not sell me dinner, sell me a great night out with no guilt when I decide to select the dessert menu
- if you are a printer, do not sell me print, sell me as many different tangible ways for people to say 'wow'
- if you are a personal trainer, do not sell me training packages, sell me self-confidence
- if you own a business centre, do not sell me office space, sell me an opportunity to build credibility, confidence, connections, and accomplishments
- if you run a networking group, sell me business friendships

If you can look through the eyes of others, it changes your perspective and mindset. As you can see from the above examples, the whole focus is on offering emotional benefits as opposed to product features.

We all want happier, healthier, and better lives, so rather than concentrating solely on the 'sale' the whole focus needs to be on 'customer needs'. Once we have achieved this, this is where we build relationships and create brand loyalty.

Defining who you are helps you stand out in a crowded marketplace. Imagine you are taking centre stage at Wembley Stadium and the 90,000-capacity auditorium includes every potential new customer with whom you would like to engage. You have the opportunity to address everyone in one 20-minute performance: can you define how you would represent and talk confidently to everyone in the stadium? Can you keep the attention of a proportion of the crowd?

If your opening sentences are along the lines of 'I'm going to tell you all why (name of company) provides the best product in the marketplace … and we have a "keep calm and follow" (name of company) A3 posters for everyone here', I can assure you that 99% of the Wembley Stadium audience will stand up and leave their seats within the first two minutes.

Alternatively, if you position yourself to the audience as providing solutions for people to live better lives/spend more time with the family/make their working day easier/reduce costs/be regarded as credible by their customers/be more successful in their marketplace, do you think you would have more people staying to hear what you have to say? Although it may not ensure everyone in the stadium will be hanging on your every word, it's going to appeal to and strike a chord with a much larger proportion of the audience.

One of the hardest things you can do as a business is to define who you are and to make your audience members aware that you exist to be of use to them. There is the potential to attract a much bigger pool of prospective customers if you are providing something of value rather than merely selling a product or service. This is where you will be able to outshine any business that is simply focused on selling a product.

Committing to building relationships with your customers will crush the businesses that try to sell by being wholly product-focused.

If your audience can define who you are, you will have the ability to build rapport; if you rely on what your product does, you will break rapport.

STAND FOR SOMETHING

You need to set yourself the goal of being head and shoulders above the competition, and the only way to do this is to stand for something that others believe in. Only then will you become a trusted source.

When other people share your beliefs and values, you can build a better relationship. If you become the same as everyone else, eventually you will be forgotten.

Communicating clearly and with a sense of purpose enables you to be understood. What is even better is that others see that you believe in what you represent and that is what helps form trusting relationships. Successful business is based on the right attitude and exchanges with people who understand what you stand for. What is even better is when others turn to you for assistance based on the trust and recognition that has developed from the expertise you provide.

Opportunities to be seen as standing for something can vary from speaking at events, to expressing an opinion in a blog. Even 140 characters on Twitter allows others to hear your point of view. These smaller conversations help others to understand your opinions, your beliefs, and your personality.

Once others recognize that you have a point of view, the shift moves from being passive to building a community that listens and responds, which is a fantastic way of becoming a visible brand. When we set out on our journeys to build a business, there was one thing that none of us ever wanted to become, and that 'thing' is being irrelevant.

Let's take the scenario of networking groups and your quest to source new business. For many networking organizations, each person in the room has a minute or so to talk about what is going on in their own businesses and share with the rest of the group. What you invariably notice is that about 99% of the people take to the stage with the same mantra of 'for anything relating to (name of industry) you really need to talk to me.' Everyone merely blends in with everyone else and the whole room becomes a cattle market with everyone looking to make a sale rather than plant a seed to connect or build a dialogue that explains why others should care.

Nobody wants to look back on their life and realize that they were irrelevant. In 2012, Australian palliative care nurse, Bronnie Ware, wrote a book called *Top Five Regrets Of The Dying*, in which she asked some of the people for whom she cared during the final 12 weeks of their lives, what their biggest regrets were.

One of the top five regrets of the dying included not having had the courage to live a life true to themselves, living the life others expected of them. Standing up for what you believe in your professional (and personal) life is not only a way to stand out from the noise and competition but is also good for the soul.

If you want to be worthy of an audience's attention, you must have an opinion. There is nothing wrong with other people disagreeing with what you state, as long as you can back up your facts. If someone disagrees with what you believe in, this helps create a further dialogue in which others can engage.

Not everyone will agree with you, but we should never set out to become everyone's friend. A defined brand personality helps attract the right audience members of which want to hear what you have to say; send the ones who are not interested in another direction; they would never be worthwhile investments anyway. Having an opinion is one of the best ways of making your brand human and achieving clarity for others about what you represent. With an ever-increasing number of businesses entering your marketplace, you can either sit with the crowd or you can stand up and make yourself heard.

In standing for something, the key driver is to educate and inform, rather than being egocentric. When others recognize what you believe in, this can become one of the strongest tools for building a brand that has credibility and recognition. Your goal as a business owner is to be useful to your audience with the end result of building a growing profit.

BUILD YOUR AUDIENCE/COMMUNITY

When business owners position themselves as the natural choice, the decision process becomes easier.

Knowing what your audience would like to know and why they need to regard you as influential is critical to being a key influencer. The more you know about your prospects and customers, the better your business is positioned to be useful to others.

There has been a massive shift for a small business toward control of the conversation and the platforms to use to build a dialogue. What is important is to understand whom we want to communicate and share with. The future for marketing your business will be based on your ability to present yourself as genuine, human, authentic, and to connect in a way that we've never been able to before. We have an unprecedented amount of spaces and places to connect with others and to present who we are, what we stand for, and to build an audience who understands our point of view.

An easy mistake to make is to think that by building an audience, you have also built a community. However, these two concepts are both completely different.

The easiest way to explain this is that an audience can be described as those people who have agreed to receive information from you. This could be in the form of a Twitter follower or a subscriber to your blog posts.

A community represents the people who continue to keep a dialogue going and transcend the customer/supplier relationship, by moving to a level of caring. This happens whether you are active within the company or not.

When I go to watch my beloved football team (AFC Bournemouth) along with the other fans, we make up the truest meaning of the word 'audience'. There are common themes to what an audience represents. For instance, the crowd shares the same interest (we support the same team), we share relevant content (talk to others about who we need to sign and who we should never have signed), we engage (shout, sing, and get into the match atmosphere), and we are consistent (we will come back again and again to support them).

Taking things into the realms of community has a different approach. Back to the football analogy, a community represents those people where the involvement goes beyond the 90 minutes of football. This includes a shared content narrative (the online football forums), rituals (going to every home and away game), and value systems (buying a season ticket, every season). The support will always be there (no matter what league or league position they are in) and will last beyond the tenure of any manager or ownership.

This is representative of what an audience and community means to a business. An audience is a group of people who share a common interest. Being part of a community has to be regarded as a privilege, where your contribution matters alongside the participation of others – but this dialogue will continue with or without you. The experience and communication belongs to everyone involved.

An audience and community are two separate entities; the definition and relevance to your business depends on what you want to achieve and build.

Being seen as approachable and doing our bit for the audiences and communities we serve, stamps the business mantra of it's not all about me, it's about you and how you are perceived.

Here is the Oxford Dictionary definition of altruism:

'selfless concern for the well-being of others.'

What I'm trying to highlight here is if we believe in a more valuable purpose than simply promoting the products or services that we represent, the perception of our audience towards our brands changes to one of approachability and having a personality that is true, believable, and above all else, honest.

This creates a brand focused on helping others and making other people's lives better. Look no further than the Waitrose 'Community Matters' initiative where the retailer supports good causes by shoppers deciding who receives the £1,000 monthly donation.

This was taken a step further by introducing the 'grow and sell' campaign where schoolchildren were encouraged with seed kits, equipment, and instructions to take the initiative by setting up stalls in stores to sell produce.

What this highlights is that any company that takes an altruist approach makes a significant leap towards becoming an influencer. When a company takes the time to be active and understand what's important to the world around them, you then position your company as one that not just sells within the community but also serves it. The future for brands is to put the ego to one side and leave this to the few who are happy to promote themselves constantly and shout out on the different social channels about how good they are at what they do. It's time to stop saying 'look at us', but rather 'how can we help?'

The altruistic brand has an audience which listens and is also happy to share experiences and make others' lives better. Playing a wider role within the community is key to being seen as a trusted resource.

A good example is the Dulux *'Let's Colour Fund'* (2012), which was set up to transform and bring colour to places that would have otherwise been left and unloved. This represents a brand not purely showcasing how good it is (overtly broadcasting) but also demonstrating how useful it can be (generating trust). In 2014, Dulux created *Colour Britain* where it commissioned illustrators to paint city murals to demonstrate how colour reinvigorates surroundings. This champions stories of heritage, history and colour from Britain.

The future success for companies is to become brands that others warm to and want to get to know better. We can all do this by contributing to the areas that we serve, or in the words of former British Prime Minister Winston Churchill:

'What is the use of living, if it be not to strive for noble causes and to make this muddled world a better place for those who will live in it after we are gone?'

Let's embrace helping our audience and our brands to play an integral role to serve a better purpose than purely selling.

Creating authenticity, passion, and building an influence within your audience is one of the most powerful tools to build support and success. Here are nine ways to be influential to your audience:

- Express yourself in a way that people will understand and want to interact with
- Stand for something that is different. If you are the same as everyone else, you merely blend into the crowd
- Target the right audience, by being seen as providing a clear solution to their problem. Is it to make their lives better? Is it to give peace of mind?
- Encourage a flow of conversation and take responsibility to listen and then interact
- Have an opinion that has clarity. It does not have to be controversial for the sake of it, but to stand up for what you believe in

As a result:

- Your audience begins to regard you as being different from other alternatives on offer and, in turn, inherently better
- Your audience can clearly see that your intentions are to solve problems, and not purely the 'sell'
- Your audience sees you as someone who is approachable, has personality, and most importantly, is human
- Your audience understands that you have a passion for your industry and are regarded as an expert in your field

MAKING A CONNECTION

The connections you make with others help solidify your relationships. This makes you the first port of call when a problem needs solving.

People are now more available than ever before. As a result, businesses that are more human establish more meaningful connections. Others feel like they can get to know your business better.

Connecting with others can drive profitability. Here is a story about my barber, a man called Terry Fry:

Terry has had his barber shop located in the centre of Bournemouth for 35 years and I'm one of many customers who still sit down, chew the fat, and have their hair cut there. I still choose to drive to Bournemouth (as opposed to a convenient walk to the plethora of hairdressers on my doorstep) to have my hair cut with Terry. It made me think why:

He greats me with a downbeat hello, not a fake smile (but that's the way I like it).

He has all the day's newspapers, neatly laid out on a coffee table.

He always offers me a coffee, before the 'what can I do for you today?'

When we talk, it's interesting. Not once have we gone on to what I'm doing for my holidays this year.

When he is finished, he always takes my coat off the coat hook and puts it on my back.

Whenever I look at the clock, I am always in there for at least 30 minutes (and there is not a lot of hair to take off these days!).

There are no 'airs and graces' with Terry, but that's fine, he is part of the old-school that genuinely has an interest in people and part of a profession where the world opens up to him within the four walls of his barber shop.

Terry's approach is something that we all need to check into from time to time, just to make sure that the conversations we have are always two-way. He has been doing this for decades and the way that he connects with others has meant that he has ridden the wave of several recessions. This is despite the increase in competition from the world of salons that have diversified over the past ten years to be more akin to 'wellbeing' centres. He has not looked to jump onto trends and widen his offering; he knows what he is good at and he has kept to it with his own charm.

What we learn from this story is that when we make our businesses approachable, we start to stand head and shoulders (is that a pun?) above the competition because that's how others see us. We need to put the welcome mat out a bit more, and by that I do not mean being at the customer's whim, by responding to every email within two minutes of arrival, but providing relief from the issues and concerns that they have and almost represent that friend they want to talk to, in good times and bad.

As businesses, we need to take the Terry approach and say: 'We know there are many choices out there, but we understand you. We are here for you and we have a track record of doing it for others who keep coming back to us, because we care.' Terry is not there for everyone, he is an old-school barber who encourages the right people to come inside, enjoy the time spent, and in a way forget you went in there for a hair cut. The brands that care should never be about jumping onto new channels that tells its audience what to do, but instead empathize with the audience and understand their needs.

Businesses, like Terry's, need to have a personality with which others can identify with and trust. When we have made this association, it does not matter how many other similar products or companies are out there. An added opportunity for businesses is that we now have an extraordinary number of spaces in which to create, participate, and be part of. We now need to adopt a faster approach and become more social. The role that content (what you say) and context (putting content into a meaningful story) play is important in letting our business thinking spread and connect with others.

Making a connection has nothing to do with achieving 'front of mind awareness' but is about your business having a deeper meaning for your prospective customers. Before we look at how you promote yourself, you need to understand the personality you want to create to communicate who you are and what you offer in this evolving world.

HOW TO BUILD A PERSONALITY
People want to work with those they know, trust, and like.

Authenticity, honesty, and approachability will always rise above the person whose only goal is to make a sale, make you feel like you've been 'pitch slapped'. Never become 'Mr Network Bore'.

This is the person you may have come across many times from networking events. 'Mr Network Bore' is the first to give the business card where its rightful place should be the bin. The focus for contact has nothing to do with looking to generate a conversation but a one-directional flow of diatribe about their business, why their business is fantastic, and why you need to do business with their company. The overlying message is purely themselves, and what you represent or the issues in which you have has absolutely no interest. This is the person whose shoes you should never fill.

'Mr Network Bore' also takes things further outside the networking event by being the person you may not have even met, but from whom you will receive an email (because you were on the list of event attendees) a day or so later with the opening sentence, 'Good to see/meet you at yesterday's event.' If they are feeling confident enough, you will also connect on LinkedIn and then let the games begin on a social platform where mass messages are sent to every connection on the merits of their business or special offer they want to put in front of you 'for this month only'.

Here are some favourites from LinkedIn that highlight a complete lack of personality and a selection of the world's laziest approaches to looking to build a dialogue.

Hi Mark,

From looking at your LinkedIn profile, I thought you might be the ideal person with whom to discuss invoicing and cash flow.

Hi,

I've sent you a Season's Greetings eCard. Click here to view:

Hi,

Hope that you're well.

I'd really appreciate if you could just take a moment to follow our company page.

Hello Mark,

I hope you're well and can excuse this direct approach.

What these examples show is a complete lack of being human. People who are devoid of personality do not entice customers into doing business with them. However, too many people forget this basic business principal. To connect with our audiences, we need to acknowledge what is important to them and create a persona that they understand and warm to.

Your brand's personality is one that should be continually evolving through the different prospects and customers you meet. Having a brand personality that has a human side also means that none of us are perfect, we all make mistakes, and if we can be strong enough to say 'ok, my fault' sometimes, then that at least shows our businesses represent being honest, transparent, and authentic.

The relationships we create are firmly built on the characteristics we represent. You need to make your customers trust you and in turn make them feel valued. Ensure you listen to them and at no point treat your dialogue as an opportunity to cross-sell, up-sell, or upside-down sell, until the customer is ready and their perception of you as a credible business is solidified. As a result, your customers will grow to understand that you're better than the competition because you make their lives easier. Instead of blending in with everyone else, let your personality come to the fore and head in the opposite direction to the competition. If you provide a clear reason why they should pay attention to you, they will listen.

The new connected world does not reward mediocrity and boredom. The biggest opportunity we all have (that was not here 10 years ago) is continuous access to our audience. You can define yourself via your personality and also portray this across the platforms you use. If you have a voice that represents what you stand for, you can blog to provide your opinion. Similarly, if your personality shines through the ability to sing, YouTube will present you to an audience you never knew existed.

Creating a personality for the business you represent is everything to do with standing out and not fitting in; it's about developing ideas and not duplicating.

A personality also means the importance of delivering a brand promise to which that others make a worthwhile connection. If you provide relevant content to your audience, members will trust you. If you fail to develop trust, your brand suffers.

When Bradley Wiggins became the first British cyclist to win the Tour de France in July 2012 (the first race was July 1903), he represented a promise built on a will to win. By doing this, he championed a sport in which British success was unheard of. The lucrative sponsorship contracts that followed his triumph were also built on the public personality he built.

A promise means that your customers count on you to deliver and you create a positive experience. Your customers chose you for a reason: was it your reputation, your ability, your delivery, your personality, or your knowledge? The positive experience that you create is something into which you have to look deeper within your business personality. We will look in more depth about being human in a further chapter.

To become a valued brand, you need to take heed of the old saying, 'You have two ears and one mouth, so that we can listen twice as much as we speak.' This phrase may have originated from the ancient

Greek philosopher Epictetus, but it is true that to become successful in what you do, you have to become an accomplished listener. By being attentive to others and listening, you create a feeling in others of validation.

PROMOTE

When it comes to sharing their messages with the rest of the world, the majority of businesses will look to self-promote as opposed to building influence as a leader.

You want an audience which is responsive to you rather than just aware of you. The way you create this is by being focused on a target market with a specific message. You need to recognize the difference between speaking directly to your audience and not just at them.

I live in a coastal town on the south coast of England (Poole to be exact) and one thing that has never been more than two miles away from me is the seafront arcades. Here is something to which we can all relate. Remember the 2p slot machines (or to the more extravagant, the 20p versions)? These are the machines where you put in the coin at the top and it could only go two ways. It could hit another coin and trigger a host of others to fall resulting in a noise of a return that would always put a smile on your face, or it can sit on its own and get lost among the crowd of other coins and leave no smile on your face. The coin getting lost among the crowd would make you relentlessly pursue a return on the money you just put in, just to leave the arcade feeling reasonably productive.

This is how the majority of businesses behave, where a message is thrown out to the different channels in the hope that there is a favourable reaction. Always remember that every single message you create has to be targeted to your audience. People need to feel appreciated and that you are talking to them, as opposed to blindly treating everyone and everything as a homogenous mass. To those who still work in this way, stop it!

When you attempt to reach everyone, the impact is small, but if you're focused and target the right audience, you create value and a guaranteed return on your investment – a bit like those afternoons spent in the arcade. If you target the right audience with an emotional appeal, not a product benefit, that is engaging and believable, richer experiences are created.

OVER-DELIVER

Providing value to others can help solidify your role as a resource that others value highly.

By over-delivering, I do not mean allowing customers to demand additional work from an agreed project to benefit them for free, but by doing the things that your competitors are not necessarily doing. This could range from keeping your customers updated with news that is relevant to their industry to the courtesy of keeping in touch after a project has finished. You grow and succeed because of the commitment you make to others, not letting them walk over you, but by taking charge and letting them know that you are here for the next project.

People like to feel connected to other people and when a customer knows this can affect the decision-making process.

Google proved this with its *Zero Moment Of Truth* research where customers purchased a product after looking at 5.3 sources of information (in 2010). Only 12 months later, this increased to 10.4 sources before making a purchase. People are now faced with a deluge of content to choose. To assist the decision process, those who can over-deliver by providing useful information that their competition does not can perhaps prompt the final selection by being seen as knowledgeable and helpful.

Over-delivery recognizes serving others on a consistent basis. In an age in which we can now entertain, show, and educate, many companies take a tried-and-tested route that has been laid in front of them since the dawn of time and is flat, uninspiring, and easily sends other people to sleep. Now is the time to grab the bull by the horns and put a reassuring arm around your prospective customers and let them know that you deliver and perform. I call this the cinema custom of 'the stretch and arm over' technique for reassurance.

Much of the allocation of time towards sales is looking for new customers, but why do managers never take note of the age-old fact that it is six-to-seven times more costly to acquire a new customer than retain an existing one?

It does make sense, in terms of costs to promote your product by selling your product to new leads, setting up new accounts and investing time, to build a rapport. Whereas, if a focus is to move existing customers to having a great experience with you, then you build a loyal following who will stay with you.

According to Harris Interactive's *Customer Experience Impact Report (2010)*, even in an economy with negative growth, customer experience is a high priority for consumers, with 60% often or always paying more for a better experience. That's an important figure to take note of where the flipside is that you lose customers because of a lacklustre service. It is time to make a stand and over-deliver to keep current customers happy (and to become advocates of your brand).

By building better experiences, your customers become a member of your community and it is important for them to feel valued and part of something. Business is built on relationships and the simple act of people interacting with and engaging with others. Here are five ways to show you care more about your customers:

1) Giving

Create newsletters that are not solely available electronically. To loyal customers, investing in great-looking printed material elevates you from treating your community as a mass to recognizing them as individuals. Back this up with a letter from you to your recipient. It is tangible when you hold a printed publication rather than looking on a screen. It still feels special and new.

2) Communicating

Communication that is ongoing. To move from purely transactional to strong relationships, put down the phone and email and connect face-to-face and create educated customers.

3) Loving

Make customers feel special. This could be anything as random as a Happy Easter card with a scratch card and your best wishes (this worked a treat for my business, by targeting a public holiday where no one really sends cards).

4) Repeating

If you do great things, it makes people want to share them.

5) Flexibility

Being flexible is key. There are times when things can go wrong. We cannot stop the mistakes that are made, it's how we remedy them that is important. Most of the time, customers want to be listened to and understood.

Every individual within your business has the responsibility to deliver, care, and to try. Valuing those around you and keeping customers as part of a community helps to create a culture where they feel part of something that they can relate to and enjoy.

(HAPTER 3

THE RISE OF THE HUMAN

Your audience is made up of other businesses that want to do business with you.

They are people who want to relate to you and empathize with the experiences you have had. It is not solely one person sitting behind a screen ready to buy a 'unit' of what you deliver.

The one thing that will always remain constant over the next five, 10, or even 20 years is who we are as people, and our online and offline personalities need to reflect this.

Although a programme such as *Klout* can measure how influential we are online, nothing will ever replace the real-life connections we make with other people. People should not think that social media platforms are here to replace interactivity. Their role is to support a two-way conversation, not to take the place of it.

The world of social media is not necessarily social. To many, it actually shields them from being public. Let's look at it this way: social media does not change anything, it's another method of talking with a long-term goal to build conversation and interaction. Over the past couple of years on LinkedIn, requests for endorsements have started to find their way into our 'inboxes' from people we do not necessarily know, e.g.:

'I'd like to request 10 seconds of your time to leave me a quick rating here:

https://mybizcard.co/user/rate/......

Thank you in advance!'

Sending a faceless message asking for personal approval to a host of email contacts who do not know you is a surefire way not building your audience. Junk mail in an electronic format is still junk mail. Distributing a templated message with a sign-off of 'Thank you in advance' lets everyone know that the individuality you once had is now replaced by a readymade email in a tone of voice that simply is not your own.

We are now overloaded with connection invitations. Your challenge is to find your own voice, be human, and become comfortable with it. The social media platforms are fantastic at building relationships and conversations, it's just a case of using them in a way that positions you as authentic and interesting to others.

Take a break for two minutes to look at your Twitter timeline and see those who are selling their product and dictating a message, as opposed to those adding value, providing information, and being useful.

People do business with those they trust. This has not changed in hundreds of years; the only thing that is different today is that we are not limited geographically. It's time to be present, stand for something, and champion being normal again.

EMBRACING FAILURE

A way to become human again is to look at failure head-on. I know it's something that can become an embarrassing subject for many people, but if we do not fail, how on earth are we going to learn? I have to hold my hands up here and say proudly that 'I have failed' (but learned from it).

When we were young children, we accepted failure as part of learning new things (think of riding a bike). It's only as we grow older and we've experienced some form of success that we learn to fear failure.

When you're doing well, it's a fantastic feeling: the invoices are being paid on time, your creativity and knowledge takes charge, and when the end of the week comes, you're ready to take on what the following week has lined up. This feeling becomes self-perpetuating, or at least until when things start to go wrong. However, the lessons that failure can teach us are much more powerful in showing us how to move our businesses forward.

Back in 2011, my business experienced a crushing blow (for which I have to take full responsibility). A customer we had been working with had begun to see sharp growth throughout their business. They were going from strength to strength in terms of industry recognition, awards, new contracts, and development throughout the whole company.

However, things had started to slip. The invoices that were once paid promptly had started to become more inconsistent: 30 days would pass, and then 60 days would pass. However, knowing the strong position the company was in, I accepted the company's responses and extended credit terms to three months. Before long, communication had come to a complete standstill. It was only then that I realized my mistake, and my only option was to turn to the solicitors.

Let's just say it did not end happily. I incurred huge solicitors' bills and the customer declared bankruptcy. I did not receive a penny from the outstanding invoices, and it put the business into a very difficult financial position. However, this experience taught me a valuable lesson about my payment terms when dealing with customers whether new or longstanding.

The lesson I learned was that my biggest weakness was trusting people too much. I now know it is misplaced trust that leads to stressful situations. I wrongly believed that the relationship I had built with the customer had made them loyal to us. Because it was a big client, I refused to acknowledge the signs that were in front of me and to act on them.

The over-reliance on the belief of future business can undermine your drive to seek out new opportunities. The only positive side of failure is if you use it as the impetus to innovate. If businesses do not adapt and they repeat the same mistakes, they fail. It is that simple.

The human approach we all need to adopt is that we should never assume we have won. We need to keep our feet firmly on the ground, keep true to what we believe, and have a clear focus on the direction in which we wish to steer our businesses.

If we can also share stories where we have experienced from problematic times, then this creates more approachable businesses. Let's face it, the 2008 recession happened and the devastation it caused individuals, families, and communities is something from which will take many years to recover from. The biggest thing successful businesses can say is that they have managed to ride the storm. However many years it takes for the next recession to find its footing, at least we will say that we have prepared ourselves and know how to cope with it. We now need to make sure we can pass these lessons on to those who have less experience than ourselves. True success is about riding the highs and the lows and being able to tell the tale.

If you can dust yourself down when things do not go according to plan, at least you have embraced the fact that you are willing to learn. If you manage and cope with failure, your business will be stronger for it in the long run, as long as you have used the experience as a learning tool. We will all make wrong decisions – employ the wrong person or launch a product that will not take off – but if we are upfront and honest about the mistakes we make, rather than hiding and pretending everything is fantastic, then at least we are considered normal.

With risk can come failure, but never become afraid of trying new things. If the world is telling you of ways to distribute emails to your audience for free, then perhaps it's time for you to try something different. Do not follow the herd; use your creativity, for example pick your top 20 customers or prospects and send them a letter in a fluorescent envelope (at least you will stand out). Rather than fearing failure, focus on solutions and not the potential problems. The execution of your idea needs to be as important as the idea itself. Failure can train us to be more courageous in work or life in general.

Stop worrying and make things happen. You have so many places to be seen and so many platforms on which you can deliver, that fear should become obsolete. Stop planning and set about instigating change, right now.

VALIDATING WHO WE ARE

One thing no social media channel or calculation can do is to make a promise to say what you are going to do for others.

Authenticity will always beat timing an automated tweet. People continually evaluate who deserves their trust. Others are able to see, from your capabilities and actions, that you operate in an open and transparent manner, only then will you be on your path to building strong relationships with longevity.

To get others to trust us, we have to earn their attention. Seeing someone on Twitter promote a blog article they've created and then putting the begging bowl out in front of them with the 'Please retweet' line is not a way to 'earn it'.

To build that affiliation with others and make it worthwhile, we all have to work hard. There needs to be a commitment to being helpful to others and sticking to it.

To earn any form of attention, others need to understand that you are passionate about what you believe in, so you own your space in the marketplace. The end result is that you become an authority and you're suddenly the person people come to respect before they even know that you're part of the space. That is when you have truly earned the attention of others, by being real and allowing people to see who you are.

PRESENT TO OTHERS WHO YOU REALLY ARE

Never hide behind a logo or, even worse, the photo of the person holding a phone close to their ear and warmly smiling into the camera to depict the '100% busy but 110% approachable' pose. Let others see the individual behind the brand (and that also does not mean a photo that was taken more than five years ago).

So, should your LinkedIn or Twitter profile represent your business or you? The answer is simple: whenever the majority of us see a profile image that is a logo, we think we are about to be sold to. A logo merely represents the company you represent, but a photo shows who you are.

People want to see individuals and one way to communicate this is by being more creative with the bio that is present on the social channels that you use. To say that you are an 'accountant', 'designer', or 'architect' does not stand out anymore and does not tell anyone much about you. You need to show others the benefit of choosing you, such as 'saving the industry from mediocrity' to 'making businesses more profitable' or 'creating leads that someone will not be able to put a lid on'. Do we really care if we read someone's Twitter bio and it says they are an 'entrepreneur'? We want people to warm to us and make a connection, we should not try to over-impress them with a low golf handicap or how productive the past two months have been.

Consistency is key to maintaining your authenticity and your social presence can help back up your approachability. Your audience now has the opportunity to connect with you on multiple channels and to find the platform that works best with you to engage with others.

People need to understand who you are and to do this you need to have created more than a good 'first impression'. To collect comments (even in the form of interviews) from customers on a regular basis (namely at the end of a project when you have delivered and it is still relevant) is a great way to show proof of your promises, attitude, and ethic. Although some companies still highlight glowing sentences (from) 'Tony' or 'Mrs P' or 'Engineering Company, the South West', the only way to bring validity to these testimonials is to show real people, with real titles, from real companies. The thing about testimonials is that the comment being shown is unique to you, a bit like your brand fingerprint, and also evidence that you've got nothing to hide.

Another element that gives validity to who you are as a person is to put a real name behind any content that is distributed to an audience. For instance, an email campaign to a section of your database always feels a bit deflating when the email being sent is from 'info@' or 'enquiries@'. What happens if you want to respond back to build a conversation?

Nobody in this world is perfect. Let's just accept that we have our weaknesses and move on. Our customers do not expect us to be automated machines; all they want from us is to show a bit of humanity and transparency alongside them.

TIME TO LET YOUR HAIR DOWN

Companies that have no defined personality will always be behind those that do. Is it not time to let your hair down and have a bit of freedom to make your mark on the world?

Let's not take ourselves too seriously; one thing nobody can take away from you is who you are. There will always be alternatives that can provide a similar service and even in some cases be a carbon copy of the product or service you provide. One thing they cannot replicate is how you do it. Let's not forget we all started our businesses with something in which we believed, from making a working process easier to knowing that you were talented in a particular skill-set.

The secret of earning trust is not in shouting that you are better than the competition or constantly interrupting your audience once they've signed up to receive information, but to be simpler and more realistic to match your claims with the audience's expectations. Being responsible to your audience helps build a perception in the minds of others.

Society is changing in that people are interacting less and less on a personal level. The LinkedIn invitations and encouragement to like and follow on other platforms presents us with a world in which we are continually collecting numbers (for the sake of it).

Putting technology to one side, we need to acknowledge that human traits will always prevail, purely because we understand more when a person connects, delivers, interacts, and raises a point of view. When others understand what you believe in – this is when you stand out from the crowd in your marketplace. The old world was about being popular by fitting in; the new world provides opportunity to stand out.

A poll by YouGov (Fieldwork, April 28–29, 2013) looked at the importance of trust, probably the most important intangible asset a business can possess. Small businesses have a clear advantage as the seed has already been sewn. More people trust small business to tell the truth when compared with big businesses. Within the 25–39-year-old bracket, 70% trusted small businesses as opposed to 17% trusting big businesses. In the 40–59-year-old bracket, 79% trusted small businesses, whereas only 14% trusted larger companies.

This is where the opportunity lies for businesses. When a company makes a human connection, as opposed to a purely digital connection, it creates an original platform upon which to build a relationship. We treat those around us with dignity and respect. People want humanity and openness, not a special offer that runs out at the end of the month.

The digital connection has its role to play in terms of the ability to build a dialogue, but when we represent ourselves and what we believe in, it makes a connection even more transparent and clear for others to understand our point of view.

THE PERSONIFICATION OF THE DIGITAL CONNECTION

The corporate voice is now being overtaken by the personal stance.

The world of celebrity has its place on Twitter and the top 20 Twitter accounts in the world all have at least 20 million followers. Of these, 17 are people and three are brands (Twitter, Instagram, and YouTube).

Sir Richard Branson's business leadership is a prime example of how a brand has been driven by an individual's beliefs. For four decades he has allowed people to get to know him and as a result we have come to trust the Virgin brand. A brand's power or share in its marketplace can be increased when it is aligned with an ethical and believable person.

The digital platforms that are now available allow people to connect with others and become mini celebrities in their own worlds. To many, the names Nash Grier and Brittany Furlan are not known, but on Vine these are people with more than five million followers and with audiences that hang on every six-second video they post. What this proves is that the more niche you are, the more you can aggregate an audience.

If you have something to say and can showcase your credibility and expertise, you can build a trusted audience, by being yourself and not following a strict corporate guideline. The world is not looking for another Starbucks; it needs you. The advice, assistance, and problem-solving you can deliver is freely available. The challenge is to build an audience which will come to you and consider you a close ally. People do not want corporate brands.

Although this book is endorsing the belief that we need to move away from heavy product or service promotion, connecting and engaging with people is all-important. To focus solely on product benefits is not a viable marketing strategy anymore. The future is about others being able to understand your beliefs and values and apply this content in the best way that works for you. A brand is not represented by a Helvetica font or enhanced by struggling for weeks on end to find a motif that you can include on a holding page/business card. A brand is represented by who you are and the story you tell.

Let's put a different slant on it. If you think that the answer to your marketing strategy is to perfect a logo and state how good this logo is, then you are wrong. While you are doing this, a competitor is already out there promoting their value to other people and explaining how they can make their lives better. The physical representation of a brand can become a very expensive exercise. Before you start, make sure you have clearly thought out your values, ethics, and principles as well as the way you want people to feel when your brand name is mentioned.

In a world in which we now have different personas and platforms trying to make you into something else, the greatest achievement is to be yourself.

CHAPTER 4

PRESENTING YOUR VOICE TO OTHERS

What makes you different from your competition is having your own voice and telling a story that is true to you. You need to stand on your own two feet and not be like everyone else.

The way to strike a chord with others is to tell real stories to which they can relate. Keep away from industry jargon, and sounding as though you are writing for a robot in the attempt to boost search results (as opposed to writing for people) as this can become a worthless exercise. It is pretty frightening to think that, one day, you may read an article that is not even written by a human and is completely automated and driven by algorithms.

When someone strikes a chord with an audience, the audience listens. We only have to watch *X Factor, Britain's Got Talent* or *The Voice* to realize the power of a story. Within the two-minute segment is a story of a situation a contestant has faced in their own lives that connects with the audience, and as a result they gain the audience's support, sympathy, or enthusiasm. Telling stories can shape our thinking and also define our individuality.

I have found that the most-read articles I have produced are those that tell a story and look to introduce an analogy with which we can relate in our personal or professional lives. These are more successful than the articles that attempt to bestow knowledge on an audience regarding how to be better at a task or skill set. Some popular articles have included how business failure can make you more powerful (this was the story of how my business hit that awkward situation a few years ago, which I mentioned earlier; it's ok to be honest!) and how the world of content marketing has a link to my failed dating past. A bit of self-deprecation thrown in is fine, as at least it shows we are all fallible and do not take ourselves too seriously.

There may be stories from your youth that still have a place in a business context. One story I like to tell others is how the world of content marketing has a link with a football team I played for when I was in my teenage years (and a very bad football team at that).

The reason my old football team and content marketing come together is that content marketing now works because of the many platforms that are available to deliver our message and engage with an audience whenever we want. A few years ago, the importance of content marketing was not recognized and so many businesses relied solely on traditional media to broadcast their product offerings. This is how the story of Canford Park FC helps set the scene:

It was a team made up of those who could not get picked anywhere else. One of the dads started a team where those kids who had not been selected for the other teams had something they could feel part of (and play for more than the 'cack handed' gesture of two minutes at the end of a game). We were called Canford Park FC and during our first season, we were known throughout the local schools as 'Crapford Park'; we had to swallow heavy defeats week in, week out, where losing 0-6 was seen as a morale boost.

However, the point I'm making here is that we were a team that decided to pick ourselves because no one else wanted us. The following season we managed to hold our own and the season after that our friends (and perhaps better players) started to join the team (our network became stronger) and we could go head to head with the more established teams of the league (and win). The moral of this little story is that all the 14–16-year-old footballers within the local borough were at different levels of ability (some way ahead of others), but when a group decided to stand for something and get better at what they enjoyed, over time it could stand shoulder to shoulder with the better teams. Other people then wanted to become part of what we stood for, which was basically to have fun.

This is exactly what is going on in the world at the moment, where small businesses are now able to have a voice and be regarded as credible alongside more established companies. All that is going on in the world at the moment is that many of us are still Canford/Crapford Park in its early seasons. We are moving away from a traditional media model to an owned media model, but are still trying to find our feet and get comfortable with it.

We now do not feel the bind of thinking advertising is the route for others to recognize our message as we can now build our own audiences and bring them to the channels that we own (our websites, our blogs, and our emails). This is what picking yourself is all about. We can now use technology to our own advantage and look to get comfortable with it, by being consistent, no matter how many knock-backs we may get and how long it takes to build momentum. This could mean a few subscribers to your blog during the first committed year, or not many conversations happening over on Twitter during the first few committed months.

As a kid, Canford Park FC represented the hopes and aspirations of a group of people who wanted to be accepted rather than feel neglected. Over time, and due to a commitment to 'keep at it', things changed for the better; the people were the same, they just became a bit more skilled at what they loved doing.

This is what is happening in the world of content marketing. Content within marketing has been present for decades, but content marketing is relatively new. Now we are starting to see the merits and capabilities with which it presents our businesses and the ability to grow a conversation and to build an audience. We are seeing content marketing play more of a prominent role.

A STORY ABOUT YOU

Your business' future depends on the ability not only to be more real, human, and transparent but also to connect.

The channels through which we can now tell our story go beyond websites and social media sites. Every interaction a potential new customer has with your brand is an opportunity to create value and to drive experiences.

One of the most important things you need to do to grow an audience which listens and believes in what you stand for is to make a connection. Times have changed from automation and repetition to originality and authenticity. Any message that is created and distributed has to represent this. Brands now need to deliver information that is believable, credible, and above all else, makes an emotional connection.

Telling a story is only part of a message. Making a connection is where the reward lies for any brand. A successful story is one that connects on a human level and means something to an audience at a specific moment in time. You need to present to your audience a sense of who you are or your point of view.

Chapter two highlighted the ability to stand for something and stimulate conversation, rather than staying with the herd, sitting on the fence, and coming across as a bland noise. This is not a popularity contest and what is important when presenting your voice to others are the topics in which you specialize and the perspective you can give to others. In a world where blogging is supporting the content overload, many sites are merely regurgitating points of view from other sites. This is accentuating a world in which many are fighting to be heard, but are merely saying the same thing. This means there is a real gap in the marketplace for you to take control. There is a tired audience awaiting someone to share something new.

Having an opinion is one of the best ways of standing out against the competition. By being the one who is delivering a different slant on things, you will automatically appeal to an audience who has heard the same message, again and again. With an ever-increasing number of businesses entering your marketplace, you can either sit with the crowd or you can stand up and make yourself heard. Let's be a bit more authentic.

No matter how many courses, webinars, or seminars are vying for your attention, none of them can teach you how to be yourself and present your own voice. Authenticity presents itself when you acknowledge your own strengths, move away from the crowd, and realize that you are unique as is the way that you do things. We do better business when we are just ourselves and do it with enthusiasm and conviction.

THE TRANSITION TO INBOUND MARKETING HELPS

The opportunity to tell our own stories needs to change as marketing is increasingly transitioning towards an inbound way of working. Let's have a closer look at the way the world was and the way it is becoming.

The traditional methods of outbound marketing (handing control of your marketing message to someone else) meant that the primary way to build a dialogue and become approachable to others was to buy advertising space or purchase mailing lists for those all-important leads and basically borrow someone else's space.

During the early 2000s, I worked for an advertising agency where one of the main accounts was a national cinema chain. Every cinema launch followed the same formula where creativity sometimes took a back seat to the 'tried and tested' paid-for media. This was basically a one-way conversation of printed newspaper ads, outdoor ads (buses, 48-sheet posters, and bus shelters), and local radio spots. This was during the early days of websites and email addresses and where people chose the local newspaper or a telephone number as the main way of finding cinema film times. This was not that long ago. Well, just over 10 years ago to be precise, but long before a tweet became an everyday expression.

The difference between the channels upon which we once heavily relied and the channels we now have, is that the old ways were extremely expensive. The term 'channel' is used to refer to the places where we distribute our messages, from blogs to press advertising to social media. The Audit Bureau of Circulations (ABC) highlighted, in 2013, that 34 out of 70 regional daily titles had a drop in sales of 10%.

The problem for businesses looking for the once 'tried and tested' route is that the advertising costs in the printed press have become more costly due to a declining readership which, in turn, reaches fewer people. It's time for businesses to rethink how they distribute their advertising message as the reach of the old routes is now in decline. It's time to look at things a bit differently as affordable technology has thrown the world completely on its head.

It's a bit like the weekly food shop, where we are all used to the routine of the same food in the shopping trolley from the same supermarket provider. Everything is in exactly the same place and we know what to expect. Sometimes, if you change your approach in terms of shopping elsewhere or altering buying habits, you can make savings or have a healthier week.

This is the same with many small businesses: the majority think they are too small to make a difference, so they stick to the readymade paths that have been formed over the years rather than making a change and altering the platform they use.

The world is changing and the increasing precedence of inbound marketing focuses on creating useful content to pull others towards your product or service. Businesses are now starting to be more interesting to others rather than highlighting the necessity of what they do. This has transformed the way we now market whereby permission-based marketing (people opting in to receiving information from you) has changed the communications process to the customer being in control of what they want to see and consume.

You now want your customers to say: 'I'd like to find out more about you, let me have a look.' This is where you can present your voice by creating information designed to appeal to the prospective and existing customers you want to target (and for them to come back and ask for more). The principles of inbound marketing are straightforward; however, understanding how to choose the right messages to portray and interest your audience can be more complex.

Inbound is all about creating content that people want to read. If we put it into context it's like the move from a speed-dating event to going out on a first (and eventual second) date.

The people who leave a speed-dating event without a date are those who look to make an impression at the early stages when the doors open. When it comes to the two-minute chats, the whole conversation revolves around themselves and their own achievements. These are the people who invariably have a disappointing evening. Would anyone want to find out more from someone whose only commitment was themselves? Those people who stand a higher chance of making that transition from initial chat to the first date are those who listen and ask the right questions. When the first date eventually happens, you then have the opportunity to get to know someone a little bit better; when this happens, there is a better chance to open up, show who you are, and promote yourself.

When putting this into a business context it starts during the early stages of getting to know a prospective customer (it could be a networking event) where you listen and then ask if the other person would like to be added to your mailing list. Over time, you may keep them posted with articles from your blog or share an eBook on a particular topic on which you are looking to build authority. Over time, a commitment to being useful, rather than getting too serious too soon, can develop with a customer who values what you stand for. The companies that fail in building sustainable relationships are those that treat automation as the norm, such as a blanket email campaign where no recipient is treated as an individual and the whole concept is to dictate.

The switch to inbound marketing has meant that we can now be influential to others by proving to be a worthwhile choice, but let other people communicate with you on their terms. The days of committing to a press ad campaign because you've had a good couple of months, or picking up the phone on a Wednesday afternoon to target a list of strangers who have no idea who you are, and about whom you know very little, is a recipe for failure. It is a complete waste of time and resources (but we've all done it with the blind hope that it will get our businesses accepted).

THEY ARE IN ... NOW WHAT?

Just because people have bought into what you stand for and understand your 'voice' does not mean that you have made it to the finishing post. Your work has only just started and all it means is that you have been granted a ticket to start the race. Your next challenge is to have a defining objective that makes you useful to others.

If you start to build a network of subscribers or grow a database organically, you have an audience which is more open to buy. Growing a database does not mean you have purchased a particular sector from a mailing company and the next step is to send an unsolicited email burst. If you choose to do this, you will find a large proportion will unsubscribe or ignore you, which is the equivalent of knocking on someone's door and the person refusing to answer, even if they are in. When buying a database of addresses, you need to remember that these are real people, not a mass of numbers that makes a particular industry look inviting to target.

When your subscribers are 'in', and stand by what you represent, this effectively means that you can spend less. The content that you produce on channels that you either own (your own website) or borrow (social media) with the aim to build an audience of loyal subscribers, negates the need for budget allocation in other areas to build awareness and affiliation with your product or services.

The king of this is the Red Bull brand, with more than four million subscribers on YouTube. This is more than one million more followers than the second-place brand, PlayStation. To keep momentum and to establish a subscriber network even further, Red Bull launched at the end of January 2013 'Red Bull TV' on Apple TV showcasing free sports content and live events.

Although achieving mass fan status on different channels is something we may not necessarily ever come to achieve (but perhaps we can at least strive for it), there is nothing stopping you building a network of subscribers to whom you have made a commitment to. In the case of Red Bull, the thing that keeps the brand head and shoulders above everyone else is the responsibility of producing and sharing relevant content for its audience. Although the budgets to cover spectacular events such as the 23-mile free-fall jump from space by Felix Baumgartner's Red Bull Stratos live stream in 2012 was akin to that for a fully-fledged film production, there is nothing stopping you from looking at more cost-effective ways of attracting others who recognize who you are and are willing to stand beside you.

The more engaged with you an audience is, the less money you have to spend on everything from Facebook ads to more traditional means of advertising. This is because you effectively have ownership of your subscribers and it is your duty to think about their needs first and to keep them engaged. This does not mean monthly product offers or 'get it before it's gone at the end of the week' sales pleas, but messages and information that is tailored to them. The biggest challenge is to promote the content that you produce while promoting your company slightly less than was once seen as 'accepted'.

One tactic that I have found that makes a significant difference is a commitment to send to my audience, at the end of every week, an email digest of news articles from the company blog. It's now a duty to serve the audience by sending them new information and stories each week, as opposed to a sporadic email on an inconsistent basis. It's a bit like physical exercise: it's something that I have to make a pledge to do every week, otherwise the week that is missed out becomes a further week missed and so on. The one thing I've learned is that relevant and owned content with a loyal following does make a difference. The following formula will help you stand out from your competition:

OWNED CONTENT + LOYALTY + CONSISTENCY = LESS RELIANCE ON 'PAID FOR' PLATFORMS

By allocating less budget to traditional platforms for promotions, you can focus on your audience effectively doing your marketing for you. This means that you are working less tirelessly to be heard and spending less on the various interruption techniques that have little or no reward. One of the biggest senses of achievement is when someone else can quote from or articulate a particular blog article that you have produced, in conversation. You did not prompt it, and neither were you looking to sell from it, but when someone else, who has not made a commitment to purchase, can share your belief, then the relationship has been well and truly formed and the ability to turn them into a customer is 95% achieved.

Your aim should be to be part of your customers' content consumption and to grow your audience via means where you have total control and your audience receives information in which it will show an interest. Your biggest commitment is consistency and time. If you add these together, you can connect with people and develop a voice of influence.

STORYTELLING

In the words of Robert Rose, Chief Strategist of the Content Marketing Institute: 'The stories that we tell are the only differentiator we have left.'

Since the dawn of time and cavemen scrawling on walls, humans have always had the ability to tell a story. Although it is important to acknowledge that people are looking for an authority and a knowledgeable resource to make their lives better, they are also looking to be entertained and enlightened. This is another element of adding value and benefitting others, by being recognized by the stories that you tell. Otherwise, you are in danger of sounding like the other brands in your industry that have no personality and nothing to say.

The more compelling the stories you tell, the more others will say, 'I can relate to that.' When you achieve this, you have allowed your audience to identify you as a person and someone they can see as genuine, rather than someone who thinks that the more industry jargon they can cram in, the more important they are going to sound. This is not about trying to sound important; it's all about authenticity and a way to bring value to others. Whatever industry you are in, you need to show that you are more knowledgeable than your competition. This could be giving an opinion on a current topic in your industry, looking at analogies to which others can relate, or commenting on market data (not product information).

Imagine that you own a cleaning company where the majority of information is based on how spotless and hygienic surfaces become (this is product information). If you use market information, the focus should now move to the customer and their wellbeing. This could be based on the fact that 80% of human exposure to pesticides happens indoors and that dirty carpets can hold up to eight times their weight in dirt, bacteria, and fungi (have you started getting itchy yet?). The objectives start to shift from where product information is centred on selling more cleaning jobs, to providing information to educate the consumer. This is intended to establish expertise and eventually build a relationship where the customer will always come to the same cleaning provider, no matter how many other choices are out there. Which route do you think sounds more likely to generate more success: product or market information?

BRINGING PEOPLE TOGETHER WITH STORIES

Everyone loves a barbeque. It instantly brings families and friends together and connections can be made with people with whom you may not necessarily be familiar.

This is an area that most businesses need to embrace, but many neglect in terms of looking to build a gradual rapport with others (as opposed to a quick win) and to create a place to which others feel welcome to return time and time again, and relate to the stories (or content) that we share.

Back to the barbeque on that warm summer's day that you have organized. When we create a place for others to come to, it's something that everyone enjoys and a time to catch up with those we have not seen in a while and cement the relationships we have and the community of which we are part. The people who are at your barbeque relate to you, enjoy your company, and trust you.

This is what businesses need to focus on: serving the community we are part of, as opposed to the desire to be popular and everyone's friend. The people to whom you have the closest ties will be the ones who will always share your content.

Because they believe in you, they will trust you as a source of information in your own right.

If your purpose is to chase popularity and to invite everyone who you know to the barbeque, then the garden will become crowded and the opportunity to talk to the people who matter becomes diluted with the influx of people who you're not really bothered about. Never chase the desire to build a community; like any relationship it takes time and nurturing. The people who you are constantly chasing to look popular develop fickle and superficial affiliations. Instead, aim to make lasting impressions that build strong relationships that stand the test of time.

A community will stay with you over a long period of time. It is your duty to be relevant to them and for them to see the passion in what you stand for. If the content that you create reflects that passion, it becomes easier for people to connect with and ultimately to share. If you create stories that are interesting, then others will want to share with the other communities of which they are part. We cannot think that the content we create is produced in one place and that is where it stays. If it is interesting to others then it will take on its own form to be shared and retold elsewhere. It is similar to the urban myths that manage to spread like wildfire. Whether it is about people waking up in a bath with a kidney removed, how a glass of Coca-Cola can dissolve a tooth overnight, or Jedi being recognized as a religion, these are stories that people love to tell. Who is to say that, on a business level, stories cannot be created and take on their own shape for others to take on-board? This is not a numbers game; this is a game where the rules are about reach. The greater the content, the further it will travel.

The ultimate reach with your content is similar to how you hear an urban myth for the first time, but others will already be familiar with it. The originator of the content has no connection to you personally, but people share it because it's good. To break into this realm of stand-out content, you have to create stories that stand alone and are then spread outside of your immediate circle built on those who already know you.

To break outside of the circle of those who understand who you are, is to never chase but to earn it through a consistent and strong body of content. This is when the barbeque can still become an event for people to come to, but the gradual increase in numbers will still consist of people who relate to you and value what you provide.

CONSIDERED CONTENT WILL ALWAYS RISE TO THE TOP

It is becoming increasingly easy for people and companies to bestow their knowledge on others. People are using the fresh technology (social) and cramming it with the old marketing principles (interruption, repetition, product-driven). What we are now doing is turning off from the information that is not relevant.

No matter where we turn, there is always an invitation to learn more by imparting your email address for a PDF; for packages to do something cheaper than the majority of the marketplace; and tweets with hashtags on a subject with the expectation that you will flock to the name of that hashtag.

The way I look at it is that although it may look intimidating that there are many others in our respective industries grabbing the bull by the horns and being continually present and churning out content, it does not mean the content created is relevant to everyone else. Well-crafted, considered, and targeted content will always rise to the top of the class because people now have the ability to filter out what is 'noise' and what is of interest.

Let's put this into the context of a real-world example. It does not matter how many thousands of people have entered a marathon, the only thing that matters is that you can run, have trained properly, and are feeling ready. Few enter the marathon with the aim of joining the front-runners and having their face on the BBC with the leading pack, but to be relevant to their audience, which is defined as the charity for which a person is running, friends, family, and anyone who has sponsored.

The way we can look to stand out from the industry competition which is quite happy creating content that is focused on its product and its own achievements via a news page that was last updated four months ago, is to differentiate to serve our audiences. Rather than creating information that is generic and just blends in with the rest, we must take a stance to educate others on the benefits of a solution and position ourselves as a provider of it. An example of mediocre content from my industry is if I were to write about what a brand represented or the difference between PR and advertising. The key message here is that creating good content has the ability to move and enhance consumer behaviour.

Providing solutions to problems helps people understand where they fit in the grand scheme of things. Instead of aiming to attract a homogenous mass, try to communicate to those who are relevant while encouraging participation and engagement. Building a strategy and message is difficult and a challenge we all need to embrace. If it were easy, then we'd all be king or queen of our respective industries. Achieving reach today is harder than it has ever been. For many of us, when we find media to consume comfortably, we continue to use this as a source of information. A good case is the increase over the past year or so in 'binge watching'. I can now count on both hands the number of friends who have watched the entire final series of *Breaking Bad* in a few sittings as opposed to the old-fashioned way of one episode a week (or worse still, all 62 episodes of *Breaking Bad* in two weeks).

We are swimming in an ocean of information overload, but, then again, we have been for decades. With advertising, PR, and direct marketing added to the content mix, the channels have increased tenfold in the past ten years. More certainly is not better, and the wish to communicate and to be everyone's friend will mean that you do not stand out at all. We don't need to be seen everywhere. Isn't it more important to be where our audience wants us? We need to concentrate our efforts on the target marketplace we can assist the best. To do this, great content engages, finds reach, and communicates in a way that builds trust and is relevant to others.

MATTER TO THOSE WHO MATTER

Your goal should be to utilize time and energy within the spaces where you deliver value consistently (and recognize limited engagement in others). Here's why it's time to matter to those who matter:

- **Monitor your analytics.** Look at your measurement tools to see where your sources of traffic are coming from. You can find this within Google Analytics in the 'all traffic' button within the 'Acquisition' section. If there are channels that are providing a limited number of visitors to your site, it can feel like the equivalent of talking in an empty train carriage, while everyone else is in the front of the train.

- **Look before you leap**. If you are going to build a presence in a new space with which you may not be familiar, get to know it first. Rather than spending time creating a profile and spending money on a new stock library image, ask yourself first, 'why am I here?' If it is because it is new and you received an invitation, sorry, but it doesn't count.

- **Prepare to be committed**. If you are going to use a new channel or platform with which you may be unfamiliar, you have to commit to investing the time. It is not a case of seeing how it goes, if you want to make a long-term impact you have to be prepared to make regular input.

- **Don't become distracted or even addicted.** Concentration takes a huge right upper cut to the jaw, when you are dipping in and out of a social channel during the day to see who has responded, retweeted, liked and reshared a post. It is another way of procrastinating and even worse is when you post an article and share it across three or five platforms, when only a couple have any real value.

- **Become more relevant.** Understand that what you create is intended for your audience which interacts and engages with you. Spending more time in the places that matter and where people have got to know you, is the equivalent of staying faithful, rather than being drawn to a new place to which you have 'taken a shine' and feels a bit different.

How you allocate your time matters. It is time to look at and monitor your armoury of tools. Just because everyone is at the same party, doesn't necessarily mean they are all having a good time. You need to understand how your content is consumed and how your audience interacts with your message.

WHY BUSINESSES WIN AND WHY THEY LOSE

Finding a voice, becoming comfortable, and recognized for what you stand for assists in the journey to becoming influential in your industry. What is central to this is the ability to sell more of your products and services.

Managing to collate a list of leads is an empty practice if you do not do anything with them. The opportunity to convert leads into customers takes time and commitment. Lead conversion is the process whereby a prospect is willing to supply information, so you can provide information and market to them. If enough detail is gathered from the prospect, then you can provide value that is specific to their needs. This will then convert them into paying customers.

These are the factors that convince a customer to buy from you:

- Prospects convert into paying customers when they hit a trigger point. This is when you've educated them so that they see the value you can offer them. It's the moment when they finally share your vision and passion and understand the purpose of what you are trying to achieve on their behalf.

- Prospective customers can see evidence of testimonials and case studies woven into the fabric of your website; this shows that you can do the job. It also proves to someone else that you have completed a similar job before and the final outcome resulted in solving a customer's problem with a positive overall result.

Once you have a customer, it's important to retain them:

- No customer likes to feel unwanted once the invoice has been paid. 'Out of sight, out of mind' does not work. They need to feel important, and ensuring a continued dialogue means they may recommend you to others. This is where the world of digital and offline can work together: tactics such as e-newsletters to printed newspapers that get posted to individuals can keep the momentum of a relationship flowing (a bit like the dating analogy I mentioned earlier: you need to keep the conversation flowing or you will never get another date).

- Cross-selling into other product areas can continue the relationship with a customer by introducing a product line with which they may not necessarily be familiar with, but can complement what they need. Customer retention is such an important aspect that follows the Pareto Principal that follows the 80/20 rule, where 80% of your sales will roughly be from 20% of your customers. The secret is to get to know the customers who are regular spenders. Remember, the stronger the relationship, the longer they will stick with you (and refer you to others).

- When customers move from being fans of your brand to loyal subscribers, then they become a key revenue source. This is where true engagement is – where a customers interacts with your brand and makes a conscious decision to invest in it financially and emotionally.

Never aim just to make a sale and move on to the next customer. People need to be nurtured, respected, and to feel part of your community. You never know what the future needs of a business are, how big it may grow, and how the diversification of your company can help people in the future.

WHY DO BUSINESSES FAIL?

According to Bloomberg, 80% of companies will go out of business within the first 18 months. Although the money running out leads to the final demise of a business, the faults that lead to this demise are in place well before the business closes.

Although the success of your business is partly dependent on your ongoing management and financial control, how you market yourself will have a significant effect on the longevity of growth you can build:

- **Take responsibility for what happens to your business**. A prime example of this can be found when watching *Ramsey's Kitchen Nightmares*. Every episode we see an example of a restaurant that has taken a spectacular nosedive and is on its knees with money owed and a family relationships in tatters. The lesson in every episode is that it's the business owner who is 100% responsible for what has happened to the business and the rocky path down which it has been taken. We cannot cling to the 'it's the recession' excuse any more (or the chef in *Kitchen Nightmares* episodes); it is a tired old excuse. Never get caught up in making excuses and realize the power for change lies solely with you.

- **Remember, you cannot do it all yourself.** Although the leadership comes from you, understand that you cannot micromanage every task and your success depends on your ability to delegate to competent and trustworthy individuals. Your role is to manage and lead those to whom you have delegated, not to manage the task itself.

I spoke to a company that was looking for a helping hand with its marketing and when it came to the message and creative delivery (as well as the sales effort), the marketing manager said, 'Well, I do all of that myself.' You cannot think that all the answers lie with one person; you have to delegate to those who are better at certain areas than you are.

It is impossible to think that one individual has enough expertise in a number of disciplines to achieve the standards that are required. Instead, seek out those who have a specialist area as this will develop higher-quality end results.

- **Understand your customer and the problems they need solving.** You need to understand what matters to them and tailor the stories that you create for them.

- **Make a commitment to sharing your knowledge and provoking thought.** Whatever tone of voice you use (friendly, conversational, matter of fact), you need to be clear about who you are, why you do what you do, and how you can help others. As the ability to share content increases, there is more of a reason to try to establish yourself as an influencer within your field.

- **Find topics that no-one else is talking about (but people want to hear).** The ease with which anyone can start a business means that there is an ocean of businesses that look and act the same. There is far too much noise at the moment and social channels exacerbate the ease of pumping content onto timelines and newsfeeds. Have a look at Google Analytics and use this to help you build an understanding of what your audience is finding interesting. This then gives you greater clarity about future topics that will be engaging (you will also find that when you produce articles that resonate, others will share them and your audience will grow organically).

- **Find your niche and claim your position**. One thing you cannot become is everyone's friend and think that your sole purpose is to keep everyone happy. You need to understand the niche within your industry and build on this. If you are a fitness instructor, the focus may be the importance of long-term health rather than solely the service you provide.

A well-known brand disappeared without a trace at the end of the 1980s since it did not understand the needs of its target audience

Sony's Betamax was introduced to the world in 1975, and a year later, JVC announced the release of its version, VHS. The rest, as they say, is history. But what was it that finished off Sony's vision of home entertainment?

The VHS format was a much simpler version and also cheaper to manufacture: a more enticing proposition for businesses to stand behind. On the consumer side, the biggest difference between the two formats was the recording length. Betamax tapes lasted, on average, 60 minutes, so just about enough to record an episode of the *A-Team* but not a film. The three-hour cumbersome videotapes for VHS were perfect to store TV programmes and films or use individual tapes to record both. It is the recording ability that is widely regarded as the key reason for the failure of Betamax. By the time longer recording cassettes were introduced, it was too late. Betamax had failed to understand its marketplace and a rival had managed to understand it better. Although the arrival of digital technology eventually rendered both products obsolete, there was once a time when VHS ruled the world and Betamax failed to grasp the audience opportunity.

This is a business lesson for us all. If you take one thing away from the Betamax vs. VHS story, it's that when the level of competition begins to increase and becomes ever more apparent, then those who have the ability to survive will adapt, innovate, and change. Those who are happy to continue with the way things have always been will put the nail in their own coffin with one swift hammer blow.

PUTTING YOUR VOICE INTO PERSPECTIVE

Honouring your audience and making sure they feel part of what you stand for, is a continuous effort in your brand fruition path. It's about finding ways for others to be part of what you are trying to create – not everyone, but the right people who fit what you stand for. The stories you tell should make the prospect or customer the hero so he or she understands the point where you're coming from. If you want attention in this world, you have to earn it first. The more you are able to position yourself as the influencer covering your industry of expertise, the greater the opportunity for credibility, trust, and profitable customer action.

The voice that wins is the one that does not shout above everyone else, but talks with others so that they can see the personality and principles behind it, and become comfortable with being part of its crowd.

If others feel confident that they can rely on your knowledge and experience, this is one of the biggest differentiators that none of your competition can possess.

CHAPTER 5

THE ABILITY TO CREATE, PICK AND GROW

What does creativity mean? Is it all about delivering something new? Is it about new ideas? Is it about having better ideas than the competition? Is it about a budget that allows you to explore? Or is it about thinking smarter?

It is important to remember to be different and be more than just a business as a means to an end, but also to stir an emotion to which your audience responds to. Well-created content comes from wrapping smart ideas around the messages you produce.

Creativity is only useful when it is harnessed in a way that allows you to turn it into an end product. Creativity is never enough; you also need strategy.

LET'S BECOME STRATEGIC

Modern business is becoming overwhelmed with a myriad of ways to deliver information, but no matter how many new platforms arrive in the next 18 months, it is the content that matters most. If you do not have a good story behind you and a reason for what you are doing, it does not matter how you deliver it.

So, how can you create interesting and engaging content?

The answer is to understand the problems that you solve for others and turn this into a series of content that is intended for your marketplace. There was once a time when there used to be thousands of markets with millions of people. Now we have millions of markets serving thousands of people. Trying to solve a particular issue in a marketplace is what leads you to becoming the industry influencer.

I have a friend called Russell who owns a printing company (everything from shop signage to bus-shelter posters). This is a very competitive industry led by price, but Russell provides useful content to his audience, from showing companies how they can install vinyl in their office, to how to make a vehicle wrap stand out.

Russell has positioned himself as the influencer in his industry because he creates knowledge-based information and shares with others.

Before the creative ideas begin to flow, it's time to take a step back and form a content strategy that you can nail to the wall and that can become the cornerstone for what you stand for. Joe Pulizzi, founder of the Content Marketing Institute, highlighted that there is a direct correlation between content marketing effectiveness and content marketing strategy.

When it comes to compiling a content marketing strategy, Pulizzi draws attention to the following areas:

1. Who is the reader or user? Ascertaining this is quite a challenging process. You may have dozens of buyer personas from which to choose.

2. What is my story? The intersection between what I know and what my customers care about.

3. In which area within my industry, can I be the leading expert that will also help my business?

4. What is the objective? Is it sales, savings, industry influencer, or customer loyalty?

5. How will I measure this exactly?

6. Is the initiative helping to build a unique audience?

7. How patient can I be in making this happen? Remember that content marketing is a marathon, not a sprint.

These seven points highlight that you need to evolve your content marketing processes and have the ability to adapt and change. A strategy is not something that is tangible or the 'answer', but a process you have to adopt to provide direction to your thinking and creativity.

Like most businesses, we all need a solid strategy to determine our goals, define our audience, and target how these are going to be resourced. What a content marketing strategy does is ensure the end product you deliver shows commitment to a cause, is consistent, and effective. We all need a path to follow, and to build our journey, we need direction. You will need to be patient at first to see the benefits of your efforts, but once you build momentum, the rewards will be more rapid and sustained.

THE CREATIVE DELIVERY

The most important thing to remember is not to limit yourself as there are no boundaries to a person's creativity.

Once you have identified and created your content strategy, it is time to take into consideration:

- within which area you consider yourself to be an industry influencer
- how your marketplace learns, consumes, and gains information
- the key message you are trying to get across (is it to save people time, is it for them to save costs, is it to make them more informed?)

If you think about how to approach things in a different way to everyone else, this then reflects onto your business.

On a recent visit to a garden centre, rather than concentrating on grass seed and the job in hand, I noted that the Jamie Oliver brand has now branched out to plants and growing your own produce. It all comes from buying into the brand that represents standing for something and living better with healthier food.

But this represents more than buying into what a brand stands for; it highlights creative thinking being a factor for success. The Jamie Oliver brand is well-respected; it is a case of applying that brand to other formats that are accepted by its audience. Creativity is a benchmark for great business and re-imagining how a brand can branch out into new products opens new markets and new audiences.

BIC took this approach by originally being recognized as a supplier of pens, but during the early 1970s introduced the cigarette lighter, and in the mid-1970s, debuted the disposable razor to the world. This is one of the leading examples of changing the way an audience looks at a brand.

Thinking about a new and fresh approach, one of the best examples I have seen was during a trip to Russia. There, they have a completely different concept of what coffee shops can offer. Take a bow Tsiferblat (based in Moscow).

Here in England, the coffee shop experience is based on paying for your drink and food and enjoying the environment (and free Wi-Fi). However, Tsiferblat instead asked people to pay for their time in the coffee shop and not the coffee/tea/muffins. This could change the whole way that the coffee shop environment is seen and perceived.

The examples here all represent either reworking a brand or a new way of working. It's about challenging the status quo and offering new alternatives that are different from the majority. Altering your approach is about trusting your gut instinct and staying true to your core belief.

THE NEED FOR CREATIVITY

Creativity is becoming the 'critical selling proposition' to everything, as described by Richard Florida in his book *The Rise Of The Creative Class.*

The only way we can stand out from the crowd is to be seen as 'artists' and follow our dreams, both in the creation process and also in delivering the final product. Seth Godin (*The Icarus Deception*) adds to this concept that we have to be unique in what we say and do because, 'If not enough people doubt you, you are not making a difference.' You cannot let traditional working rules hold you back. Marketing has shifted rapidly in the past 15 years, arguably more than any other business discipline. The rulebook now needs to go out of the window. We simply cannot rely on the traditional textbooks to tell us how to behave and sell within our marketplaces. Not only do we now need to make a stand but to be successful we also need to be innovative, remarkable, create stories that spread, and have a clear human approach. These are the traits Godin described of 'the artist'.

One thing that is prevalent in the connected economy is the increase of 'shiny new toys' to play with (but is an app going to make us more productive and interact better with others?).

These 'shiny toys' are all of the social media platforms that want us to interact, converse, rate, share, and be part of. We still see many instances of Twitter being used as an interruption tool to boast and LinkedIn as a platform to gloat, rather than as mediums to help, advise, and add value to their target audience's lives. The problem with communication platforms lies not necessarily in what you say, but how you say it. What many businesses fail to understand is that technology does not necessarily make working processes easier. What you get out of it depends on what you put in.

Technology can provide you with untold advantages when it works for you, but always remember that just because a piece of technology is available to use, does not mean that you should step up and use it. Take a bow QR codes. My favourite place for seeing a code to scan was on Twitter for a local property developer. To encourage people to visit its site, this developer asked its audience to use the same mobile device they were using to read the tweet to scan the code! If there is a parallel universe in which this is easy to do, please let me know. Let's just say that I did not rush to open my Mac and then scan the code with my mobile device, because I think we can all guess that something not very creative or engaging was on the other side of the link.

Just because someone scanned a QR code does not make it a successful strategy to adopt. However, if the idea is to be creative and encourage someone to visit a specific landing page or a mobile site with engaging content, rather than a homepage where it is just as

If you ever need a quick click to our page don't forget the QR code #buildingdorset pic.twitter.com

easy to type in the URL, then this is where QR codes can be useful. It is all down to how you use the medium. Make sure that your goal is to encourage others to interact with you. It's the same with all technology: things work when they are used properly.

Many business owners are not trained or encouraged to be creative and make communication platforms work for them. Why should they if their key strengths are in other areas? To many, it is a case of getting the 'toy' and diving straight in.

The majority of business owners do not have any formal experience of using technology or being creative about how to distribute messages across various platforms. In their keenness to use these new applications, people fail to adapt to a new way of working and cram traditional ways of marketing (repetition, broadcasting, and interruption) into new applications. This means that any opportunity to create a meaningful dialogue with an audience is lost.

Sometimes, it's just a bit of creative thinking, the right application, and the simplicity of an idea that goes beyond any popular digital platform. Take, for example, this message for my local sandwich shop, in Poole. There was a very unfortunate accident when a

car was parked nearby without the handbrake on. The owner stepped out of the car, without realizing the handbrake was not applied, the car rolled down the hill, and crashed through the sandwich shop window causing untold damage.

The damage was clearly evident where the once pristine shop front window was replaced by plywood boards (for a good few weeks). But to everyone who passed the sandwich shop it was not the boards that were the talking point but the 'drive through application rejected, business as usual' chalkboard that was outside the shop.

This simple device (a chalkboard with a chalk message) meant that, despite the unfortunate accident, the sandwich shop received extra exposure, from coverage in the local press to blogs.

Sometimes, it's not a case of jumping on what you're told to use because everyone else is using it, but embracing the power of an idea. Creativity will always trump conformity; it's up to us how we deliver our message.

TIME TO PICK OURSELVES

The days of fitting into a corporate culture because our parents told us to get a 'proper job' are no more.

Many people have lived their lives waiting to be picked by others. From the school team to the job interview, we've been educated to believe that we need to be chosen by others and conform to their way of working, to fit into a box and become accepted. Not being chosen has always left us with a sense of rejection. Missing out on being selected for the school team, not being invited to a birthday party, being turned down to 'go out with' in favour of another friend are all ways in which we have come to accept rejection in our everyday lives. The key thing here is to unlearn these behaviours in which other people hold the power. Instead, we need to be focused on picking ourselves first: once we make others see how much we value ourselves, they will, in turn, come to value us as highly too.

Not only is it important to broadcast a positive perception of ourselves but also to be adaptable to the environment around us. In the words of Alvin Toffler, author and futurist, (1970): 'The illiterate of the 21st century will not be those who cannot read and write, but those who cannot learn, unlearn and relearn.'

The world is evolving so that technology, the economy, and the ability to build an audience has changed everything. People are now using this to their advantage to learn and to grow. Businesses are now picking themselves in an age in which technology, art, creativity, business, and passion are fusing together to create opportunities for true wealth (that is, more than money).

Picking yourself provides more freedom for your creativity to flow and generates ways of getting a reaction and affiliation with your audience. Musicians now use YouTube to grow their exposure without 100% reliance on record labels. You only need to remember Psy's *Gangnam Style* (released in 2012), which broke the *Guinness Book of Records* for most likes on YouTube. If we go back further a few years, to sites such as MySpace (remember that?) musicians such as Lily Allen and Arctic Monkeys saw the benefits of using this platform as a springboard for their success. By uploading their songs they were able to build a mass fan base while the record labels remained reticent to invest in new artists.

Whether you are an aspiring Lily Allen or a fledgling business, building recognition starts with realizing the talent you possess and the power of making platforms work for you.

By allowing others to have access to what you produce and easily interpret what you deliver, you can build a loyal audience. You no longer have to stand up against a wall with everyone else and wait to be picked. You can stand aside from everyone else, develop the ideas you have, and deliver them in a way that is meaningful and different.

Another example of someone picking themselves is comedian Louis CK. He is one of the shining examples that show you do not need to have spent money on marketing agencies to promote and share your product.

In 2011, his Live At The Beacon Theatre *performance was distributed exclusively via his website for only $5. In just 20 days, downloaded copies grossed more than one million dollars. From being rejected on* Saturday Night Live *in the early 1990s and finding his way through the stand-up circuit for a decade, to finally having complete control and an audience that was receptive to what he delivered, Louis CK showed that you can control the media on your own terms.*

To have a fan base that stick by you, on your terms, is one of the most powerful tools you can have to reach others (as also seen in the music industry with artists such as Pearl Jam and Radiohead).

OVERCOMING THE FEAR OF REJECTION

To accept rejection and believe that you can make a change in others is a trait you need to develop when deciding to choose yourself. The fear of rejection is in us all, but once we learn to harness this, it can help us set the foundations for who we are.

Let's go back to my school days and look at where it started for me. I liked a girl for the best part of a year when I was 15 years old. Finally, an occasion arose when I could put my master plan of 'wooing' into action. It was a basketball match against another local school (having a height advantage over a lot of others had its benefits as I was effectively the person to whom everyone passed). I knew that the girl I liked was watching, so I let this become an occasion to show off.

With my cocky confidence sky high at the end of the match (I remember we won by a couple of points), I went up to the girl in front of her friends and asked if she *'would go out with me'*. The response was pretty unanimous where the girl laughed at my question and she replied *'not a chance'* in front of everyone else (and her friends then told me *'she already has a boyfriend'* to rub it in a bit more). This heralded the start of day one in understanding what 'rejection' was.

Rejection is one of the biggest obstacles we all have to face when it comes to standing for something and shaping what we represent as people.

The other angle is what if you never try? At least rejection shapes our perception of the world. If we aim to steer clear of rejection, we run the risk of ending up with a life or business that is bland, too scared of trying things that are not necessarily in our comfort zone. The individual experiences of rejection I have had in my life have been too many to remember. We all get rejected, because we are all different people; from those who do not appreciate what we have to offer or have done for them, to those who are not willing to see our point of view, the important thing to remember is that it is the learning that comes from these experiences that helps make our businesses stronger.

The only thing that lets you rise above rejection is losing the fear and accepting who you are. If you try over and over again, at least this shows you have 'spark' and that you are willing to try new things, rise above the rest, and have a foundation of resilience.

It is now easier than ever to become stuck in a mindset, where we can not free ourselves from the shadows of rejection. Facebook is a prime example of this, and in 2013, the University of California looked into the effects of 'digital dumping'. The studies showed that a third of people interviewed (24 people aged between 19 and 34) could not bring themselves to delete photos from their social networks following a break-up – many people find it hard to let go.

To embrace exclusion whether on a personal or professional level, is to ensure the foundations that you have built are resilient and that you are happy to accept who you are and what you stand for (on a physical and emotional level).

This also sets the precedent for having a voice that is yours and is worthy of being considered by others as influential, by expressing an opinion, and being unfazed by rejection. We all need to have a viewpoint and whether people agree with it or not, all you need is to make sure you have the evidence and the belief to back it up. Let's face facts: not everyone is going to like you, all brands are human, and all humans have to make judgments. If we can be present, not shy away when we head down a road with which we are not familiar, and stand tall, then we can build better and more influential businesses.

In today's world, those who take responsibility are given responsibility. When you connect with others you create value.

Many wait their entire lives to be picked by others (such as employers or clients), which can hold us back, rather than looking to select ourselves. Technology now lets us share our opinion, prove that we can help others, and carve a niche audience which believes in us.

The opportunity to create a community via a website and have a platform on which to blog can be a great opportunity that can transform any business. It helps to aggregate an audience that understands what you stand for. As businesses, our goal is to make ourselves indispensable in how we serve others.

In the days before the social web, we had barriers in front of us. The people to whom we wanted to reach out were hidden behind HR walls and paperback books (authors.) These walls have now come down and we can interact with other people more easily than we ever have done. Others can now see that you can solve problems and provide solutions to your marketplace.

The tools with which you need to be armed today are: energy, knowledge, consistency, an email account, a computer, Wi-Fi, and an abundance of ways to reach an audience. Forget the work/life balance, people who pick themselves find the right blend between personal life and work.

When LinkedIn rolled out its influencer programme in February 2014, the gates opened for all users to contribute (instead of being restricted to the most influential – the likes of Richard Branson, Barack Obama, and Tony Robins). People with a voice and a story to tell now have the ability to reach an audience they could never have previously imagined.

We are all now owners of media companies that serve audiences. Businesses can now reinvent themselves by utilizing the media (meaning the places where they can control and distribute a message) to demonstrate knowledge and entertain others. The thing that businesses need to remember is that everything that is created has to have meaning, otherwise it just becomes a pointless distraction.

Consumption of media is changing. Accenture's 2013 Video Over Internet Consumption Survey *highlighted that watching TV is not what it used to be. The average viewer across the UK, France, Italy, Spain, Brazil, and the US still watches TV, but they are accessing content using a range of other devices and interact with others during viewing. A total of 72% watched video via a laptop and 63% have consumed video via mobile devices or internet-connected TV during 2013. What this presents to businesses is a clear opportunity. Whether this is to stand for something via a blog, create regular video content, or become consistent at podcasting, the barriers to entry are virtually zero. The greatest investments we need are our time, appreciation of the media that we are using, and becoming committed to a media platform to deliver consistent value.*

We cannot make something for everyone anymore and one thing we do not want is to be chosen by a mass market. Our goal is to put something in front of others that they will talk about and share, something that may facilitate change and make their lives better. We do not want to do work that's popular, but work that changes people. The three things you must identify are:

1. Who your audience is
2. What you will change
3. What work you will deliver that will make a difference

For our businesses to become noticed, we need to take responsibility and break away from the masses. From the *Start Up Britain* stats highlighting the year-on-year growth for start-ups (see chapter 1,) marketplaces have become far more accessible to entering as has taking ownership of them. Before it starts to become more difficult to find your place, you need to identify your niche audience from an early stage.

TIME TO GROW

Most companies fail to progress because everyone else is doing the same thing they are. If you manage to create and deliver something for your marketplace that fills a gap or need, the path to success is pretty much laid out in front of you.

Businesses fail because they create a product or service merely because they are able to and the barriers to entry are low. What they deliver is just another carbon copy of other businesses, with a similar price and distribution method. To grow, businesses need to do something that others are not doing. If it's a way of looking to build closer relationships, it's what makes you different that enables others to take notice and begin to care about you.

Once you have found your style, then you start to make a step out from the world of ordinary. If you cannot fit in, you now have unparalleled spaces to create and share your approach with other likeminded people. Gone are the days of repetitive chest beating and tone-deaf communications based on companies listening to their own voice with a lack of understanding for an intended audience. In its place is creating meaningful communication that can take you places where you can collaborate and co-operate with real people.

The ability to grow is about creating connections on a one-to-one level and the various platforms that we use to distribute our message. Our lives are being publiscized every day via the phones that are in our pockets within every space that is around us. Thinking that interrupting with product messages is the future is completely wrong. We need to become better storytellers by understanding how people connect with one another. It takes time, but when you've got it right, you build influence by creating meaning in what you deliver.

Growth happens when you make an impact on others, sending tremors that are felt by those outside of your immediate audience. We can leave an impression on those people who matter and over time, others will gather around us. If we take it for granted, then what we are looking to build can crumble. This is exactly what happened to a project on my house.

A loft conversion was an ideal way to create more space in my house. Having met a number of builders, my wife and I selected a company that had a track record and was run by someone with whom we made a connection and trusted. The final loft was just as we imagined: more space, a great finish, and something of which we could be proud. When friends started mentioning they were looking for new building works, without hesitation we recommended the builder. At the very end of the project, the final invoice resulted in an extra £3,500 for works that we had not been made aware of. The goodwill began to fade and recommendations were soon overtaken by warnings: 'I would not 100% trust this builder, they are not very transparent.' The impact was made, but in the totally opposite direction. Our group of friends have shared a number of tradespeople over the years from painters and decorators, electricians, to the handyman who can construct IKEA wardrobes in no time at all; the work has been shared among people we all trust. Instead of increasing trade for this company, when our friends began looking for builders, they went elsewhere.

According to White House Office of Consumer Affairs, a dissatisfied customer will tell between nine and 15 people about their experience. About 13% of dissatisfied customers will tell more than 20 people.

A lesson for all businesses is that to become recognized and grow, every single interaction you have with a customer has an effect on your brand – the resulting effect is either positive or negative. We all want to be remembered for the things that we did right, no matter how large or small. From an email exchange, to a blog, to a one-to-one conversation, our brands are always presented to others with the goal of building a relationship. A single poor experience can result in a customer lost forever (let's just say that the future conservatory project is being discussed with another company). Every opportunity we get to spend with a customer is a great opportunity, or in the words of management heavyweight Peter Drucker, 'Quality in a service or product is not what you put into it. It is what the customer gets out of it.'

Keeping things on a home improvement level, whenever painting needs doing I always stick with Claire and Sam (who were suggested by a friend a year ago). These two women have always helped out via their painting and decorating company, which has always provided a service where they've been upbeat, understood the job in hand, and been happy to provide recommendations for the best paint to use (and an email cost confirmation within a couple of hours of their visit). Their work has been recommended to many others and from painting murals on garages, to painting nurseries, they've become well-known within my network of friends. What we see here is that once a sale is made, the opportunity to create brand advocacy begins where we know to whom to turn when we need a helping hand. What Claire and Sam sell is not painting and decorating but an experience that gives peace of mind and ease. It is these experiences that makes it easier to recommend to others. It's not necessarily the massive things where we focus time and strategy, but grasping the little things that can matter. This can help to stimulate interaction, deliver a strong product or service, and a fruitful relationship.

The ability to create, pick, and grow represents new and innovative ways to nurture a place where others need you. The future has nothing to do with depending on others, but others relying on you. The businesses we build can become untouchable rather than cowering in a corner when a handful of poor-performing quarters result in a company-wide cost-cutting exercise. The opportunities for businesses are to be recognized as publishers of information where we create and curate content that our customers love, appreciate, and that make them want to stand by us.

CHAPTER 6

BUILDING YOUR MEDIA COMPANY

So far, we have looked at what you need to do to become influential to others. Now let's look at the opportunity you have with the content you create to think and act like a media company.

Every business has the opportunity to gain trust, earn attention, build an audience, and convert consumers into loyal customers. Every company is a media company. People consume content that is relevant to them. With the increasing number of messages that are tugging at our sleeves for attention, we are becoming better at filtering information. This means the information that resonates with us will be from sources that we trust and approve.

Media sources have been around since the 15th century: the introduction of the printing press (by Johannes Gutenberg) enabled the mass production of books and dissemination of knowledge throughout Europe. Gutenberg's print press was also credited with printing the *Johan Gutenberg Bible* (of which two copies can still be found in the British Library).

A media company can be defined as a business that produces informative content to build an audience.

This definition stands the test of time. It has been with us since the advent of print, the ability to record and broadcast (with gramophone records) during the late 19th century; the introduction of cinema and radio during the early 20th century; the beginning of television in the 1950s; the evolution of the internet during the 1990s; to the mobile revolution over the past 10 years or so.

Over the years, we have consumed all these different types of media from reading a magazine to binge-watching every series of *24*. This is the same for our businesses. Everyone you know has an email account (and even more traditionally, a postal address) and at least some presence on social media channels. As we take things further into the 21st century, you can now reach further than ever imagined. You have a host of media tools to add value and to aggregate an audience. The purpose of media is to reach people, wherever they are; from sitting in the comfort of their own home, to being crammed on public transport, companies can distribute information whenever they want. Please do not think that bombarding someone with sales messages is going to get a result, it simply is not.

We are now in an age when we can create content that strikes a chord with others (be it written, filmed, or audio). We can distribute across any platform that we have nurtured and developed (email, social, website, newsletter).

For businesses to become successful in propagating their own message, they need to begin to act like media companies. The biggest strengths small businesses have over their larger counterparts is that they can be faster, more social, and create a voice of their own. Speed now wins.

Small businesses have logistical freedom that larger businesses do not have. There are no barriers to procurement, PR, or a tiered decision process before a message is distributed. Even better, it is easier for others to get to know a small company's personality. Whether you take the approach of a formal, straight-to-the-point or a more relaxed tone of voice, at least people can acknowledge what you stand for and your humanity.

When you make that step to embrace becoming a media company (and your personality is defined), you can manage the content you produce in a flexible way. The control, creation, and distribution of information requires a skilled approach and it is down to you as a business to identify what works best for your audience and the preferred formats you produce.

The biggest change in the world of marketing in the past 10 years has been continual access to an audience. This is such a powerful opportunity, but can be easily mismanaged by an approach that is bereft of strategy or meaning. Many companies still take this approach, and have nothing interesting to say. They show a total lack of personality and humility that serves only to alienate themselves from the audience with which they connect.

Success for businesses today is down to the ability to adapt and evolve as the world progresses. No one can predict what the future will bring. Similarly, when looking back before 2007, could anyone have predicted the impact Apple's iPhone would have on the way we consume and share information forever?

Everything is moving faster. According to *Search Engine Journal*, 72% of all internet users are now active on social media channels and 93% of marketers use social media for business. Without going into too much detail relating to large numbers and drastic change, everything has stepped up from a leisurely run to the realization that everyone else has been training for a marathon. What you have to accomplish as a business, is to understand what is relevant to your audience. People now have the ability to filter out the noise that is broadcast from their TVs to their mobile phones and to absorb what is meaningful to them (and on their terms).

To step up and be regarded as a media company is a long-term strategy as opposed to a 'tried it for three months and it did not work' mentality. A successful mindset is about longevity and the platforms that suit you. More importantly, it is about the ability to re-educate, relearn, and apply.

We all have to adapt as people and businesses that consistently learn. Becoming a media company involves looking forward instead of reducing where you are currently.

You cannot sit comfortably with where the world is now, as the end result is that you will think and behave the same as everyone else. You have to find a place where the market is heading by staying abreast of current trends and becoming committed to your learning pathway. If you aim to achieve this, you will always stay one step ahead and by the time others have caught up, you will have moved on.

One of the most famous examples of not understanding the direction in which a marketplace was heading (that eventually resulted in the demise of a company) was when Netflix offered to sell itself to Blockbuster. In 2000, the fledgling company looked to build a dialogue with Blockbuster to form an alliance and become the streaming side to the business. This also meant that a 49% stake in the company would be sold (so it would still be called Blockbuster). The sale price was $50 million (today's valuation is about $20 billion with more than 36 million subscribers), but this was flatly refused. Ten years ago, Blockbuster believed that customers loved the experience of walking into a store and browsing to decide what to watch as it had real tangible quality to it. We all know the ending to this story!

There will always be companies that will keep their feet firmly fixed to the way they have always done business and not realize that the world is changing. We only need to look as far as Woolworths and its stance of selling pretty much everything. Woolworths wanted to appeal to everyone (selling everything from CDs, to pencil cases, to birthday cards) and did not really have a firm grasp of its target market, whereas Wilkinson, The Pound Shop and The Card Factory got to grips with theirs. The world of pick-n-mix sweets does not ensure a sustainable marketplace and businesses cannot look to be all things to all people while technology and consumption habits begin to change.

The principles of the marketing mix's 5Ps are still very important (people, product, place, promotion, and price), but we all now consume content and messages in a completely different way from how we used to in the 20th century. To be more specific, we now consume in our own time. The days of sitting and watching TV in real time are long gone. When I watch TV, it's via 'catch up' even to the point where I use the TV to watch YouTube (which gets me thinking are we now watching TVs or computers?). The consumption of media today is in a completely different hemisphere to 60 (no, make that 20) years ago, where heavy thinking, planning, and implementation was a staple process to broadcasting a message. Today, speed allows us to control and story-tell in the real world and adapt to the different platforms and techniques that we use.

We are living in a cultural shift where authentic engagement has superseded product promotion and interruption. The old way of battling for attention is still rife on social channels and the web, blogs, and email, but platform mentality is slowly changing.

Businesses are now learning to respect their audiences a lot more with real intent and also consider the spaces that audiences use. This is the world we are now starting to embark upon. Storytelling and having creative freedom allows us to act with authenticity. We cannot stick with what we've always been used to. We need to know the places where our respective industries are heading.

Businesses have to adapt. Many others will be happy to regurgitate what has been handed down to them and do things the way they have been told to perform them. What has been passed down from generations of inertia is not in line with the seismic shift that has happened within the world of marketing and business over the past 10 years.

When you stop becoming an enthusiastic learner, competitors will start catching up with you in less than a year. Businesses have an opportunity to study how to influence a marketplace and become influencers themselves.

YOU ARE A SELF-PUBLISHER IN YOUR OWN MEDIA COMPANY

Taking things to the next step, having a media company you control means you are a creator, curator, and self-publisher.

The digital world is now dominated by the relevance of meaningful content. To Google, you are just as valuable as *The Times* when the content produced is appropriate and credible. We can all now publish information in either an online, or printed, format and it can take the look of whatever we want it to reflect. What a position we are all in, but what's stopping us grabbing the initiative?

The challenge is to create and to own your space. Every company today needs to be a media company in the way that it provides key information to its audience. According to Jupiter Research, relevant emails that are targeted to a specific audience drive 18 times more revenue than broadcast/sales-based emails. As media companies, you have to understand what is relevant to your audience. What works is to put yourself in the audience's shoes and identify ways to make members' lives better. What questions are they asking? What difficulties could they be having at the moment? What is stopping them from making a leap from where they are, to where they want to go? It takes time, but once you understand your audience you can connect. Once you've connected, you can repeat with a proven formula.

Audiences now want information on their terms; it's up to your business to know what makes prospects tick and deliver information in a useful, compelling, and engaging way.

A WAY TO THINK ABOUT YOUR ROLE AS A MEDIA COMPANY

Your role as a media creator and distribution outlet is now part of your company mindset and personification of what you do.

Imagine that your business is a weekly magazine that sits on the newsstand. Within that newsstand is a mix of other titles aimed at different audiences. One thing we do not do, and will never do, is to read every magazine that is on the shelf (this represents the overwhelming amount of content that is in front of us every day). When you take a step back and analyze the genre of magazine you want to read, the magazine titles and front covers are what draw you in (this could represent everything from your website homepage to e-newsletter).

It has already been made clear earlier in this book that we are not aiming to appeal to everyone or race to be 'popular'. Instead, we want to be relevant to the audience which is interested. The content that you produce should never be aimed at everyone. Similar to the magazine that is your business, you want to create something that makes an appeal on an emotional level and encourages a personal connection. What you want is your reader to come back to you for the next issue.

As a media company that has a weekly title to attract an audience, it is now your job to create content that is relevant to your audience that is informative, thought-provoking, entertaining, and useful. You need to put yourself in your audience's shoes and identify the content that appeals to them. When you think of your business as a magazine title, it becomes easier to understand the necessity to build an audience. The goal should be for your readership to feel compelled to find out more, interact with the magazine, and make the decision to subscribe. To take on the role of editor within your 'magazine' (which in relation to your business could be your website), you need to take responsibility, authorship, and make decisions that maintain and grow readership figures. If the magazine is filled with far too many adverts (or in the real-world context, self-promotion about how good your company is), eventually your audience will become tired. They will know what they are buying into is something that is filled with limited information and a heavy amount of promotion.

When people read your magazine they want a mix of article scope, stories, opinion, interviews, reviews, education, and most importantly, to be entertained. This is exactly the same as your business where you have the opportunity and responsibility to grow an audience by creating content and distributing it across the platforms on which you want to be represented. This could be via blogs, video, podcasts, email, guides, and social media.

Why not take a few minutes to write the title of your magazine.

Note: who is the audience that will buy the magazine? What will it look like? What type of articles would the magazine cover? Is it easy to get in contact? How do you want your readers to interact with you?

If you can collate your thoughts and understand where you'd like your magazine to be positioned, you are on your way to creating your media company.

OUR NEW WORLD

The world was a simpler place when businesses were driven by a campaign mindset; where we could propose and schedule an advertising campaign, and work on a relevant aspect of print to promote a message (from direct mail to full-blown brochures). Now, everything has changed because our eyes and ears are shifting to more places.

What we are all moving towards is the screen that is in front of us or as president of Twist Image, Mitch Joel, highlights in his book *Ctrl Alt Delete*: we live in a 'one-screen' world. We have all been used to the traditional three screens that have been with us, namely TV, computers, and mobile. The one-screen world is not a possible trend but an inevitable movement that has already taken place.

Let's look at it this way: whether we consume content with our tablets, phones, or TV, in a world of simultaneous device usage the only screen that matters to you is the screen that is in front of you. According to Ofcom, there are 83 million mobile phone subscriptions in the UK (the last recorded UK population measurement in 2012 was 63.3 million people). If this highlights one thing it's that mobile usage has erupted. Visits to retail websites through mobile devices have now overtaken traditional visits by desktop for the first time, according to *IMRG Capgemini Quarterly Benchmarketing Report (2014)*; 52% of retail visits were made via mobile, and 36% of UK sales are now from smartphone or tablet devices.

Joel highlights that the one-screen world will become commonplace due to a whole host of factors including: the affordability of smartphones; consuming music, TV, and books. It is becoming easier to access content, and people are now more comfortable watching video clips and TV shows on smaller screens.

So what does this mean to you and your business? Business owners need to grasp how technology works and how it is evolving (even if this is a scary concept!). Although one day we will probably be overtaken by robots, we all need to understand the role that technology plays now and become aware of how it can shape our businesses. From using apps to making our social presence easier, to making sure the websites we created are optimized for mobile devices, to understanding the best ways of reach via email systems, the platforms that are available to us continue to grow. Remember that it is only through embracing these new technologies that you can have a clear strategy that keeps your business current and moves it forward. The content that you create, and search engine visibility, has to be a focus for the strategy that you undertake.

If people are using the screen in front of them to search, make sure that your content is discoverable. You should not be absent from your marketplace merely because you have not embraced the technology that allows people to find you.

THE CONTROL YOU HAVE

Having control is not just about what you do now, but what you do in the future.

Every business that wants to make that leap, can now have complete control over the process of creating, curating, and distributing information to aggregate a targeted audience to drive sales and long-term relationships. The reliance on traditional methods such as newspaper advertising and buying lists for a direct mail campaign have shifted from the reliance on places that we rented to spaces we now own (from print, digital, social, and more). Having complete control means ownership is now in your hands and we can alter, mould, and enhance customer behaviour where they pay attention and are interested in the information that we produce.

Imagine you are in a pitch to a potential customer for a 12-month retainer contract. Throughout the day are the time slots for the other businesses and before you walk into the boardroom fresh with the smell of aftershave, you see the previous company walking past you and you catch the eye of one of the 'other' pitch team. You can be sure that 99% of the companies that have pitched have delivered polished presentations that highlight the merits of working with them. I should know, as throughout the best part of the 2000s, this was the formula that my business and previous businesses I had worked for used, from brands such as multinational beverage company Diageo to national museums. Being the company that becomes recognized throughout the pitch process is not about waxing lyrical about the competencies and merits of past successes, but delivering in that presentation information that is relevant to the potential customer with the aim of making them feel more knowledgeable and more successful by making a more emotional connection. Sure, the testimonials, and printed collateral for the pitch with the date on the front cover have a time and a place, but telling engaging stories that are relevant to you and the meeting in hand will always supersede self-serving information provided by the other pitching companies.

Having control of the information that you produce is not about twisting a perspective and being relentless via one sales channel but making a person acknowledge, think, and perform differently.

AGGREGATING YOUR AUDIENCE TO YOUR MEDIA COMPANY

If you can convert a specific number of prospects to customers, you can truly focus on who matters and forget the time wasters who take up your energy and resources.

Our goal as businesses (and people) is to earn a living and maintain growth within niche markets. I'm now going back to an article here from the 'dark ages' when the iPhone was not even a year old, by Kevin Kelly, founding executive editor of Wired *magazine. Kelly wrote, in March 2008, a famous article that stated that all we need is 1,000 true fans to make a comfortable living.*

Kelly stated: 'A true fan is defined as someone who will purchase anything and everything you produce. They will drive 200 miles to see you sing. They have a Google Alert set for your name. They cannot wait till you issue your next work. They are true fans.'

If you build 1,000 customers and find that space within the media landscape that is relevant to them where they consume information to help them consider and buy, then you effectively never have to do any more marketing; not a drop, it's done. Rather than saying that a huge number of customers need to be found, a realistic and manageable number needs to be a business' ultimate goal. It relates to the idea that we need to change what we are doing and focus on those people who matter.

Although I'm not saying that Kelly's article is the magic formula for businesses to build an audience and then stand back and watch customers continually come forward, his comments about building a loyal audience do add a realistic angle to selling to those who matter. Although we are not going to become the next Amazon, whose content is minimal but which gets customers who always come back for more, it does help us to see the importance of focusing on an audience and understanding who the customer is.

We cannot build our 'fan bases' quickly and think that the 'this is the last chance I've got' *X Factor/Britain's Got Talent* approach via a plea is the way we should operate. When businesses do this, they run the risk of facing a heavy fall. The business world example of this is everywhere. Just look at every 'Please like our page on Facebook' message, or 'Please retweet', or 'Download our free report' prompt. The begging bowls are prominent throughout every channel and places that we visit.

The main lesson to take from Kelly's article is that, as businesses, you need to focus and address a market that is receptive to your message. This becomes the factor to determine success or failure.

Let's make things even more straightforward by explaining our businesses in terms of a lighthouse. The role it plays is to guide ships to shore rather than attract every ship in the sea. A momentary loss of focus could lead the ships being steered into the rocks.

This is a principle that can be applied to your businesses. Rather than looking to attract everyone within your marketplace, focus on those who matter, the people who rely on you for guidance and whom you trust. If you are looking to attract everyone, at some point the control you looked to maintain is overtaken by a sprawling mess of becoming all things to all people. Focus is completely lost and eventually, there will be only a few who continue to turn to you. The word here that stands out above everything else is 'niche'.

If you are looking to control your niche and become recognized, there are a few factors to take into consideration and apply:

- **Use technology to your advantage**
  It is not good practice to be on every social site purely because everyone else is. If you do not think that you will be very active on Pinterest, do not use it. Select the media platforms that you will be committed to and embrace them.

- **Create a specific solution for your audience**

If you can be associated with providing an answer to your marketplace to make consumers' lives better, then you become the source of information rather than part of a mass of other products or services.

- **Pick a subject to represent**
  Rather than becoming part of a glut of information covering a vast array of topics, find those subjects that are representative of your business and have interest to your audience. For instance, if you are a print company, do not start veering down the world of recruitment.

- **Understand the audience persona**
  Segmentation is key to grasping how your audience reacts, behaves, and their personal attributes. If we are all in the business of working with people, we have to know who they are rather than trying to target everybody.

- **Create content to build a framework**
  Produce information that is not only engaging but to which your audience can relate. You need to drive a response from prospects to subscriber to customers. Set the momentum for creating a benchmark and commit to it. Once content is created (written, spoken, or video), it has to add value to others.

- **Build membership**
  People want to feel that they are part of something. If someone has taken the time to subscribe to your site, then treating those who want to build a closer connection a bit differently can work. Rather than sending a message to your subscribers and then ten minutes later the same message is seen on every social media space, make sure those who want to be part of what you do, feel as if they are. They are in your space, so treat them well.

- **Community development**
  Giving purpose to what you provide and taking this to a wider scale to benefit others (to educate and give back what you have learnt) can help add credence to what you stand for and the personality that you deliver.

- **Connecting on a personal level**
  If we are to play the long game, let's become more human and interact with others. One person who does this with his weekly e-newsletter is author, publisher, and blogger Chris Brogan. His subscriber list must be many 000s, but his Sunday message that is sent to everyone's 'inbox' has a personal level to it. Every email is addressed personally and the content is down to earth and makes you feel like you are sitting in the same room as him.

- **Find a rhythm and maintain the conversation**
  There is nothing worse than committing to an audience with various forms of communication and then stopping. This is all about being fit and conditioned to run the marathon, rather than being unprepared and failing after the first few miles.

  To build an audience which will stay beside you, you cannot simply target anyone with a pulse. It's the answers you provide and the ease with which you deliver to others that makes what you do compelling. Coming back to Kevin Kelly's seminal article, businesses need to inspire others to make a change, and once a rapport and rhythm is built, a strong bond is created.

- **Creating your platform and distributing via your channel**
  Before building your space, let's take a step back and look at the definition of a platform and a channel.

THE PLATFORM
The broadest definition is that a platform represents the place to

communicate an idea and to build a dialogue with your audience. It is where you are visible to others.

The difference from 10 years ago to today is that the number of platforms upon which you can communicate has now increased tenfold. Platforms are now available to manage social networks fully and also respond directly to customers through the platform (such as Twitter).

Managing complete content marketing operations can also be supported via programs such as HubSpot, HootSuite, Adobe Social, Contently, and Kapost. These allow us to create content a lot more simply for the websites that we build and maintain via open source sites such as Wordpress and Drupal (as a guide, users publish more than 40 million posts a month according to wordpress.com).

THE CHANNEL

A marketing channel represents the vehicle delivering your message.

Only 10 years ago, the platforms we used were limited in their means of communicating (although straightforward for the media buyers) compared with today's world. For brand launches or new campaigns to attract the largest possible audience, ad spend was focused on outdoor advertising, radio, TV, press, and direct mail – how times have changed!

Fast forward to today. For a business to build an audience, it first needs first choose the appropriate channels. Websites no longer necessarily need a heavy investment to build and maintain. You can now:

- build a discussion and listen into competitors/prospects/customers via social media channels
- create and share video content
- build databases where the ownership is yours (which is as simple as using an Excel spreadsheet)

When the use of a channel is successful, it enables high-quality connections where the audience appreciates the value you provide. By focusing on these connections, you can then begin to form a trusting relationship. You do not have to become an expert in it all, but instead need to have a space that you can effectively own and is authentic.

Since the start of this century, the sophistication of new media channels has completely changed the way in which we interact with others via:

- websites
- blogs
- email
- e-newsletters
- mobile
- search engines
- social media
- e-books
- webinars
- video
- customized printed magazines/newsletters
- apps
- podcasting
- events

WHAT DOES DISTRIBUTING MEAN FOR YOUR BUSINESS?
One thing to remember from everything highlighted in this book is that committed, consistent, and relevant communication to a targeted audience aids the decision process to ultimately purchase from your business.

According to a DemandGen Report, nurtured leads produce, on average, a 20% increase in sales opportunities versus non-nurtured leads. It is our role as businesses to develop and implement a strategy that keeps engagement levels consistent until prospects are ready to make that move to become a customer. By implementing the tactics highlighted from the various channels (and we will look in more detail at some key areas in the next chapter), you can increase the probability or the rate at which this can happen.

SOW YOUR OWN SEEDS AND CULTIVATE YOUR OWN SPACES

It is becoming ever more apparent that we have to sow our own seeds, rather than rely on what has already grown.

As cultivators of content and information, we have to take greater control of what is ours, by not overusing the places that belong to others. It is now time to take greater ownership of the digital spaces that we own (our email, blog, website). It is becoming increasingly apparent that the doors are shutting elsewhere, or you have to now 'pay to now enter'. Anyone who thinks that Facebook or Twitter is a place owned and controlled by them is naive. If anyone has ever taken the time to go through Facebook's 14,000-word terms and conditions, they will realize that the content published on the site is available for others to use whenever and however they want.

Although we all agree that these free services have made our lives easier and made it quicker to share our voice with our audiences, they have to be paid for somehow. Social media platforms are not a charity, they are here to utilize the information we provide. Building your platform on someone else's terms is not the way to create an online arena.

The most important lesson for us all is to market within our own digital spaces as though no 'helping hand' exists. We depend so much on others to drive our own business results (for example when we look for acknowledgment and rely on others to share), that we can neglect the fact that one of the biggest opportunities we have as businesses is to create value. Remember that if you publish content within your own spaces, you have complete control and no-one is going to disable a feature or start to charge you for 'entry'.

We need to create a hub rather than search for spaces that are already well-worn. Development of our blogs, websites, and email are the answers for sustained growth. If we can emphasize what we stand for, other people will feel compelled to come on board and share our point of view. This sets the foundations upon which to grow from our own land, and for others (prospective customers) to consume what we produce. As an example, email is still the most reliable platform with which everyone is familiar and understands (according to the Direct Marketing Association, there are 3.3 billion email accounts compared with 1.73 billion social network users). You could say that email was the first ever social network with which we became familiar.

Any social channel that we are currently using heavily can be turned off tomorrow. We used to be drawn to Facebook because everyone else was; now they are looking to charge us for the privilege. We cannot grow on land that does not belong to us. This is emphasized brilliantly by Sonia Simone's *Digital Sharecropping* article on Copyblogger.com in 2011, where she highlighted:

'If you're relying on Facebook or Google to bring in all of your new customers, you're sharecropping. You're hoping the landlord will continue to like you and support your business, but the fact is, the landlord has no idea who you are and does not actually care.'

In the rush to become social, we have all become impatient, by looking to build business recognition and credibility in the shortest timescale possible. At the same time, businesses are losing a grasp on what it takes to market a product or service, and being distracted by the choice of available channels. We need to become a bit more thoughtful, committed, and consistent within the spaces that are ours. As small businesses grow, the initial patches of land that were modest in size, start to develop. Through dedication, hard work, and ingenuity, over time the dependence on others becomes less frequent.

For your plots to grow, you need to imagine the content you create is part of an allotment. To be successful, you need to have a mix of:

- **Light:** This is the content you create that is shared with your audience on a frequent basis or the times during which your audience is exposed to what you deliver to.

- **Space:** The seeds you sow (or the content you create) has the ability to be recognized on its own merits. This is contrasted with sounding like everyone else or what the industry has dictated throughout recent history.

- **Sowing times**: Some seeds like to be planted during different seasons throughout the year. Similarly the content you create, there are times during the year that you can take advantage of. Maybe the end to this year is going to be the year when the posted Christmas card makes a resurgence rather than templated GIFs sent to contacts.

- **Fertilizer and different types of soil:** Some plants are OK in weak sand. When translated to a business context, this is the ability to create content that is not too time-intensive. Some plants may need compost and regular fertilizer to keep them strong. In the business context, the longer-form content that has a longer shelf life can be translated into different formats and repurposed. From an initial blog article, the idea can be adapted to form a piece of creative for print, or a design might become a part of a video.
- **Feeding:** Make sure the allotment is constantly fed with both sun and water. To make sure the spaces that you have control of

become bounteous requires an amount of patience, dedication, energy and commitment.

- **Tend to the plot on a regular basis:** If shortcuts are taken to fast-forward growth (with a bottle of 'Miracle-Gro') then long term, this makes the plot of land unsustainable. You may see short-term rewards when growth is supported 'artificially', but when the emphasis is devoid of drive, passion, and attention, then long term, growth will stall.

Your audience needs to recognize that you are here to deliver useful information that does not have a flashing 'SELL' sign above it. As a result, over time, your small plot of land can become a more accepted space where others want to consume what you grow and share it with others. You cannot rely on others all the time to help you deliver what you set out to achieve. Remember that your ultimate aim is self-sufficiency.

WHAT YOU NEED TO REMEMBER

To become a media company, you have to remember that you already are one – this does apply to you! What you need to do now is to accept that:

- You can and should provide value to others (with the end result to drive profitable action).

- Your audience will consume information via the channels they prefer and the technology they prefer to use (laptop, tablet, mobile).

- The way that media has traditionally been distributed has altered. The once-limited number of available channels has now exploded to more affordable ways for businesses to utilize.

- Real-time news breaks in minutes, not days, and businesses can now act on this, using what is relevant within their industry.

- Audiences are continually tuned in – from coffee shops to making the morning commute bearable. Mobile devices will only continue to grow. According to Morgan Stanley, estimates are as high as 75 billion connected devices by 2020.

Having a commitment is the essence to becoming a successful media company. In the words of Joe Pulizzi (in his book *Epic Content Marketing*), the creation and delivery of information to a targeted audience is about *'owning media as opposed to renting it. It's a marketing process to attract and retain customers by consistently creating and curating content.'*

The way we consume information and our purchasing decisions have changed. Consumers no longer respond to forced messages and lists of product benefits that some businesses continue to provide. Instead, buying behaviour has changed to reflect the wealth of information that is available digitally about a product or service. Now, many purchasing decisions will start with a Google search, looking at industry-related articles, along with reviews from other consumers.

To progress is to accept that your business is a media company. The challenge is to become disciplined to create, curate, and distribute content on a consistent basis that is relevant to your marketplace. Only when you have become successful at this can your business become a trusted resource that educates and entertains others in its own right. To attain this, your delivery needs to provide solutions, opinion, and discussion. It is a role that will need ongoing nurturing and development to ensure you continue to build momentum.

CHAPTER 7

TOOLS TO REAP THE REWARDS

A mindset needs to be embraced that:

- educates others to buy into what you stand for

- creates a relationship where others value your opinion

- creates engaging content to generate profit

Previously, a mindset to push a product to others (the town crier) was once accepted as the norm. However, the whole premise of this chapter is that, in today's market, to drive profits, you actually need to become a teacher.

Businesses that still engage in ways of working driven by a hierarchical system (where business is dictated from the top down) are causes for concern. In these companies, pressure is simply passed down to the levels below and everyone feels the weight. A prime example of this is the mis-selling of PPI from high-street banks during 2013, where staff were ruled by targets set by others. Although the pressure on staff to achieve these targets resulted in initial profits for the banks, in the long term this has cost them millions in compensation.

Instead, businesses need to learn, adapt, and evolve a new way of working that suits them and their consumers. The future has to be about how to change our way of thinking, communicating, and marketing our products and services.

The attitude baton now needs to be passed from relentless selling to concerted education. To be stuck in a tired old wheel that is based on a faceless approach to selling where integrity, engagement, and belief comes second to a corporate hierarchy of 'the way that we've always done things here' is a recipe for failure.

Businesses now need to adopt a more purposeful role and teach others. Competitive advantage is created through the ability to share knowledge and encouraging others to think for themselves (throughout the decision process). Presenting yourself as an educator provides an opportunity to share what your business represents while furthering discussions on a one-to-one basis. This can strengthen relationships, build rapport, and encourage empathy from your audience so they identify with you and what you stand for.

Integral to the role of a teacher/educator (someone who is happy to share knowledge and expertise) is the ability to create a discussion that directs others. The media that is now available provides an opportunity to facilitate a dialogue that engages with others and enables them to reflect. The content you create can draw others towards you by establishing you in a role of guidance rather than purely a role of transaction. The result of this will be that you will become seen as a 'trusted advisor' – not someone who knows all the answers – someone who is able to work with others and strives to improve learning for themselves and others within a particular field.

THE FORMS OF MEDIA

To become a better teacher to your audience, you need to adapt your message across the various channels which people consume. The mistake many businesses make is they use the same message and repeat it across all channels. This involves no modification for the audience and does not adhere to the etiquette of the channel being used. For instance, you cannot cut and paste the same message that is used on Facebook (that is more than 140 characters) to Twitter (where posts are 140 characters or less).

Although this chapter focuses on owned media, there is still a place for combining a mix of paid and earned media to create an integrated programme of activity. Historically, many businesses have a heavy skew still toward paid media. Let's define the three tools to set the scene.

PAID MEDIA AND NATIVE ADVERTISING

Paid media is traditionally paying for advertising to gain presence for a brand in the place where consumers are spending their time. This is also used as a driver to owned media properties. An Altimeter Report (2012) defined paid media as a 'form of advertising for which a media buy is necessary'.

This has led to the content explosion of native advertising to build engagement with potential customers. Native advertising relates to placing content within the context of a publisher's site. For many businesses, the quality of content and relevance to the consumer is superseded by paying for advertising with branded content within a space that is owned by someone else. The whole purpose is that the content should be identical to the tone and voice of the publisher and be of interest to the reader. What native advertising should not be is a media approach to camouflage overtly promotional messages within editorial content.

Whether the name of paid or native enters the conversation, to sum up the 'father of advertising' David Ogilvy, 'What really decides consumers to buy or not to buy is the content of your advertising, not its form.'

EXAMPLES: print, web, television, radio, direct mail, outdoor advertising, paid search (pay per click), sponsorship, advertorials

EARNED MEDIA

The most common description of earned media is in the principles of PR, where businesses spend a great deal of time looking to build a relationship with editors, journalists, and publishers to facilitate stories relevant to the media title. In simpler terms, brands have the opportunity to promote themselves without paying for advertising to gain credibility (perhaps through word of mouth), with the aim of reaching more people than via a paid media strategy. Recently, the dominance of social influencers and bloggers is recognized as a source of earned media.

EXAMPLES: media relations, word of mouth, organic search, video, social media posts, viral content, reviews

OWNED MEDIA

As you become your own media company, owned media refers to the content over which you have complete control and which is maintained by you. The emphasis is to have ownership of the spaces over which you have responsibility (your email, your website, your blog) rather than the places where you have partial control (social media pages). The principal aim is to nurture relationships and extend your brand presence beyond your website (where control is still with you, for example printed communications).

The shift to engaging directly with customers can encourage long-term relationships via regular activity. According to the 2013 *Brand Keys Customer Loyalty Index* (surveying more than 39,000 customers), emotional engagement is the main driver for purchase decisions rather than traditional tactics such as discounting and price promotion.

EXAMPLES: email, newsletters, website, blog, mobile, video, podcasts, webinars, infographics

YOUR CHALLENGE AND RESPONSIBILITY

The challenge is to create and own our spaces. According to Jupiter Research, relevant emails that are targeted to an audience drive 18 times more revenue than broadcast/sales-based emails.

As a media company, you have to understand what is relevant to your audience. You have to put yourself in members' shoes and identify how they want to be served and what matters to them. Once you understand your audience, you can connect. Once you've engaged, you can repeat with a proven formula.

Audiences now want information on its own terms; it is up to businesses to know what makes prospects tick and deliver information in an informative, compelling, and engaging way. Your competition is now starting to open its eyes to how the media landscape is changing. You need to be wide-awake and be one step ahead.

A 14-YEAR-OLD'S APPROACH TO CONTENT MARKETING

I am now going to regress to a time with which we can all associate. It was before the world became too complicated and we all got too serious. Here are two ways to explain why a content commitment is a route that can deliver tangible results. Let's go back to when you were 14 years old.

THE GEOGRAPHY CLASS

The opportunity businesses have to become media companies, with the focus on an owned media approach, has its roots in a geography class.

An effective content marketing approach mirrors the flow of a meandering river that had its place in many school textbooks.

Without taking things too far and moving into the realms of explaining how 'ox-bow' lakes work, let's put it into a principle of a constant flow of content and a growth of material(s) that can stand the course of time. It can become a clear analogy to work with.

THE FLOW & GROW CONCEPT:

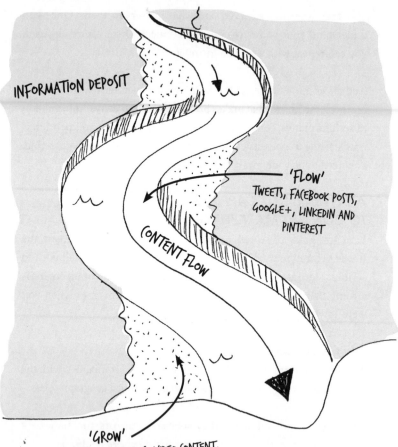

INFORMATION DEPOSIT

'FLOW'
TWEETS, FACEBOOK POSTS, GOOGLE+, LINKEDIN AND PINTEREST

CONTENT FLOW

'GROW'
BLOG ARTICLES, BEST PRACTICE GUIDES, VIDEO CONTENT, WEBMAILS, IN-HOUSE MAGAZINES, NEWSPAPERS AND E-NEWSLETTERS

The flow of the river represents continual movement towards the mouth of the river basin. In terms of content, the frequent flow of tweets, LinkedIn entries, and Facebook posts represents the continual stream of activity aimed at your audience. The flow of information is always intended to reach your target audience. If the flow of content starts to become more sporadic, eventually the river basin will become dry.

As you can see from the diagram, the flow of the river produces layers of sediment deposited on the side of the channel. Within a content analogy, the deposits represent more substantial, longer-term, and more useful information that is produced. Rather than the frequent 'flow' of information, this represents the ability for content to 'grow' and to stand the test of time (and be recognized as more substantial than a train of thought).

The sediment deposits represent the high-quality content from: blogs, best practice guides, video content, and in-house newspapers/magazines. These are all directed to help turn your customers into knowledgeable influencers (within their marketplace). This is the more considerable material that represents a greater investment of time. More time-intensive content is designed to represent a deeper level of learning material than the continual flow of information.

The concept of the continuous 'flow' of information and 'growth' of more considered content cannot work in isolation. As is found in the river diagram from the school textbook, the flow of information over time helps contribute to the distribution of sediment throughout the river channel. Taking this to our content metaphor, the regular short bursts of information can help contribute to the longer-form content. For instance, a tweet can help form the idea for a blog, and a collection of blogs can then fit into categories that can help develop the material for an e-book or industry guide.

The entire river can represent our aim as businesses to be perceived as a trusted resource. The route to become recognized as the preferred business choice is never a straight line. It takes a concerted investment of time and energy. What the 'flow' and 'grow' concept represents is a commitment to consistent quality.

To sum up, the analogy shows that the continual flow of content represents a commitment to create and distribute information. If the river stops flowing, the once steady stream of current becomes a barren riverbank. Likewise, if your commitment to embrace sharing knowledge and conversation becomes a sporadic input of empty tweets and irregular blogs, then the rich source of information becomes obsolete and irrelevant.

By continuing to invest in your brand and build trust and rapport with your audience, you can become a trusted influencer. If this becomes the focus, rather than purely interrupting people with the merits of your product from 9 am to 5 pm, selling becomes a lot easier.

THE PAPERBOY

The role social media plays in a content marketing approach is similar to that of the role of a paperboy.

Your website represents your key platform of information and the main source of content. The channels you use form the distribution of information (where the link should always come back to the primary source). This is where the full story is and its role is to engage with your audience.

This is similar to the job many of us had as teenagers, where delivering newspapers on a freezing winter morning was a weekly occurrence.

Let's get even more nostalgic, as this could also be a link to playing *Paperboy* on the Commodore 64 (or taking it a few years after, a Nintendo Gameboy).

The bag within which all the newspapers are tightly packed, represents the principal source of information. The streets of houses are either those people who have subscribed to receive the newspapers or the houses on the road that are not interested in what you are delivering. The movement from each house that has subscribed, includes the preference for media consumption for each household.

Let's take a look at this in a content marketing context. Your main website where all information is located and measured is the base for all information. When we move into the realms of social media, this represents the distribution of short links that should always reference back to the origin of the content. Always remember, social media should never be used as the primary source of information from which key content originates.

More substantial material such as blogs, video, e-books, and guides all form part of the main source. Although social media is integral to the success of a content marketing approach its main aim is to fit into the context of the main message, rather than being the core message.

To sum up the metaphor, the bag of newspapers represents the main source of information (your website), the houses on the street receiving the newspapers on a regular basis are the people who follow you on the various social media channels, and the type of newspaper received is the channel that each person has decided they prefer to consume (Twitter, Pinterest, and so on).

THE FOCUS

Businesses need to move away from outdated marketing methods. This includes putting the eggs in the advertising basket or believing that buying a list of names of strangers is going to buy customers and longevity.

The purpose for the rest of this chapter is to highlight the marketing tools that allow you to have complete control. This means you will not be affected when the owners of particular channels start to charge you to have a potential dialogue with an audience (as mentioned in the previous chapter).

The following pages are dedicated to your website, your blog, and your email, as well as discussing the role of print (which is not dead, but just needs to be used more creatively).

YOUR WEBSITE

Before anyone makes a purchase decision, your website is the place where people will go to collate more information. A website is a necessity for doing business, and making it mobile-friendly with a responsive design (so rendered correctly for mobile and desktop versions) is becoming the norm.

Your website is the source of information and the heartbeat for how you communicate with the world.

Take a leaf out of Google's book when it comes to being regarded as the source. When you visit Google's homepage, you will see no content, just the rectangular box to enter what you are looking for. Google then comes back within seconds and lets you know the sites that you might be interested in to look further. Every time you want to know something, you always go straight to the source. What is stopping your business from being regarded as the authority within your industry?

The principal factors are to become more open and more honest if we want other people to look at us for reassurance. If we share what we have learned and become more widely regarded as an education provider and not a conduit for solely delivering a product or service, we can become a valuable source of information. Your role should be to help others and point people in the right direction.

Make your website abundant with information rather than product-heavy jargon. The days of a website as purely a selling tool are over. Consumers are wise to it and people are looking for what matters to them. Remember that the only person who cares deeply about your company is you. Thinking that the website news page covering project wins, new work, the charity day, the profitable last quarter, and new staff appointments will compel others to buy from you, left the station in 2009. It has no use to anyone else, whatsoever.

Everything that your prospects or customers read has to have them in mind and understand the frustrations that they encounter every day.

A website is not about regurgitating the pages from a printed brochure and pronouncing the excellent level of customer service, which you deliver. What your website needs to be is regarded as a resource that you want to encourage others to revisit. When the time is right to make that step to purchase, your prospective customer is already primed with what you do and how you help. Your website is here to attract and engage others and to provide a wealth of information in which they will be interested and is relevant to them.

GETTING DEEPER WITH CONTENT

Creating information that is readily available, but serves a deeper purpose, is something that can position you as a trusted resource with an honest voice. One project I created was something aimed purely at my local market where the content would be shared within the business community.

I wanted to talk to a number of business owners who were well-known within the local area (in terms of longevity and having built successful businesses). The purpose was to get them to share their knowledge based on 'If they could get in a time machine (back to where their business career started), what three things would they advise their younger self.' The audience was small businesses with an aim for them to learn from those who had grown their professional careers. The answers were to be collated and an e-book was to be created for others to download.

The book involved an investment of time in terms of collating the interviews and creating the eBook (which was a PDF download at ifyoucouldgoback.co.uk). Although the e-book was given freely, people were asked to leave their email addresses to access the download. This meant that the time I had invested in the project had a return of growing my audience – which was interested in the things that I had to share.

Since the participants in the project were local, rather than send an email and wait for a response, we met up face-to-face to have a conversation. The downside to this was that it took a huge amount of time to edit and prepare, but the end result was a database of new contacts, who had opted in to the company database. The e-book eventually became a free download on the company website (www.theidgroup.co.uk).

Although building the database was important, what I wanted to do was create a valuable piece of content for others to use and take from. The end result was exposure on a wider scale including radio interviews, local news coverage, and building relationships with contributors I would never have had before (a kind of reverse cold calling exercise!).

Feel free to use this idea and implement it within your business. The aim is to become influential within your market as an honest and informed resource. The main lesson I learned is that you have to make the participation as easy as possible for each contributor.

SHOULD YOU GIVE AWAY CONTENT ON YOUR WEBSITE?
If you give away content for free, it encourages your audience to see you as an honest and selfless authority within your industry.

Do not become a hoarder and keep your expertise in storage. If you do this you will be of no value to anyone and your business will suffer as a result.

Let's look at it this way: you are far more likely to attract customers if you are offering to teach something that is of value to them rather than simply selling your product or service.

People are now faced with an avalanche of content from which to choose. To assist the decision process by providing information that your competition is not currently offering, can prompt the final selection in your favour by being seen to be approachable, knowledgeable, and helpful.

Your business goal is for others to regard you as influential. You can create an open approach to share information for the benefit of others. If you do not give generously, then someone else will. This means that someone else has the opportunity to build a dialogue on their platform while you are guarding what is precious to you.

A conversation I had with a software provider was that my company website should have more landing pages for our guides. We should also be more dominant throughout the website by requesting email information to push the sales process from prospect to customer. However, people are now becoming more conscious of leaving personal information. There has been a number of instances of personal data being stolen (such as 4.6 million Snapchat usernames and phone numbers hacked and published in 2013). People are now more wary of leaving details, let alone being bombarded with 'buy from me' messages.

On occasion (where there is a heavy investment in time to produce specific content, for example the guide highlighted previously), it is appropriate to ask for personal information – in most instances, making content freely available is always the best route. Although giving away content cannot be measured in terms of who supplied their email address to access, what it does provide is a greater opportunity to be:

- shaped (you control what you want the communication to say)
- shared (you decide through which channel to distribute the message)
- spread (downloaded from outside of your immediate sphere of influence)

Why create obstacles and reasons not to download when you want others to understand your point of view and something on which you have spent energy and time?

My company requested email information with our local business project purely based on the time taken to interview and produce the final report. Three months later, when this guide was placed freely on the 'resources' section of our website, downloads had increased by 25% within the first month of it being freely available.

We need to humanize how we work and encourage others to trust us. This does not work via the one-off '*Ten ways to be a thought leader in your industry*' report, but to be consistent and to build depth in your knowledge. People will be more willing to become part of your audience if they know that you share useful resources.

If you give away content, understand that the world will not suddenly be filled with a host of other companies who do 'what you do' – sharing your knowledge does not give away trade secrets to your competition, or enhance what they do in any way. In the marketing industry, there is nothing that is unique – we all just do things a bit differently from one another. The biggest contrast is that businesses package up what they do in their own ways.

The key to giving away content free is to change your mindset to one of generosity and having visibility in your approach that is relevant and useful. If you give away content for free, this will always slay the company that just wants to sell its products or services.

THE BLOG – MAKE YOUR OWN RUCKUS

Your website is the source for everything that you deliver and the starting point for the problems that you solve. Businesses, and more importantly individuals, now have a louder voice. This enables you to showcase your thinking. You can start your own movement via a blog, which is another space over which you can have complete control.

Let's just start by saying that I am not a fan of the word 'blog'. It has moved on to different levels since it was introduced as a 'zine' and built popularity during the late 1990s. The impact and importance of this method of communication has taken on a new form of resonance as a 'learning resource' for an audience to consume. What is stopping you from blogging and becoming the best teacher in your industry? Why not take an approach where the content you create has an educational slant for your audience? It is time to focus energy here rather than on the 'about us' or 'news' section of your website.

The easiest way to approach your blog (or 'learning resource' as I prefer to call it) is to consider it a continual development of your thinking and the approach to how you work.

If this is prompting an inclination to make that leap, remember that everyone has to start somewhere. This means being comfortable with creating work that you can look back on and acknowledge that you have developed your own thinking over time.

EMBRACE THE RUBBISH YOU CREATE

It can be a bit embarrassing looking at where you started. My first tweet on April 1 2009 was, 'First entry. I must embrace this technology … not Facebook but Twitter ahoy'. (You can find your very first tweet at allmytweets.net.) The early days were a mix of finding myself on this new channel and broadcasting what can only be described as nothing of much value.

This is similar to the early months of creating blog articles: you have to be committed to finding your own path. It is important to become comfortable with writing and expressing your angle of opinion. It does not happen overnight, it needs an investment of time (and in the grand scheme of things, that's not such a bad investment).

The 21st century has so far highlighted that writing is becoming a skill that we all must possess. Most of our content is now consumed online and represents a global shift whereby we are absorbing what we read on our phones, tablets, and computers. Although most people cannot claim to be revered copywriters, writing is a skill we need to embrace for our products and services to be recognized and to create better results.

Finding a tone of voice and pledging to write, means that you can create better content and tools of persuasion. Creating copy and sharing helps make a stand rather than passively consuming and reading what others have to say while you quietly sit in the background. If you can accept that, during the early days, what you write might be lacking in inspiration, that is fine – over time this develops if you make a commitment to writing.

GET YOUR BLOG WORKING IN THESE STEPS

If you have not taken the leap into the world of blogging, here are some pointers to help you get up and running. The objective is to help shape your voice within your marketplace.

KNOW YOUR PLATFORM AND DESIGN IT WELL

Remember this is all about having a platform where ownership is 100% with you. Although the likes of LinkedIn's publishing platform and Medium are attractive in guaranteeing further reach, these are sites rented from other people. In terms of reputation, WordPress is the perfect platform for writing longer-form content. Once you become comfortable with creating articles, there is always that satisfying feeling of pressing the 'publish' button. When it comes to hosting and setting up the blog, although there are many themes to use it is always best to have someone in place who has the knowledge and expertise of creating WordPress sites. Otherwise the effort in creating a well-presented blog can look a sorry, time-consuming mess. Design your blog well; no one ever got excited about and engaged with a blog that was slow, unresponsive on mobiles/tablets, and looked unloved.

CREATE YOUR BIO

Too many people skip this. At the end of every article you produce, whether on your site or guest-posting on another website, make sure that the person reading it is able to find out a bit more about you. Do not slip into corporate waffle, but highlight the areas that you specialize in. There is nothing wrong with a bit of humour for others to recognize that you are writing from the heart and not like a robot. Make sure that your contact information is always present (and links to other sites where people can read more about you).

DISCOVER WHAT IS THE TRIGGER TO WRITE

It is always the most difficult step to begin writing when there is not much content to fall back on or a history of articles. The best tip is to read regularly.

When I made a commitment to reading things started to change. You start to become more creative and strategic with your thoughts. My preferred choice is still to buy a hard copy of a book. Writing notes as you read becomes an easy reference to come back to and for about £10, you are given a wealth of knowledge to think about and apply.

It is easy to be distracted by reading through Twitter and LinkedIn posts and clicking through to read articles that strike a personal chord. It is a bit like going for a run and thinking, 'I will stop for a walk when I reach that lamp-post.' It just does not make you feel that you have pushed yourself and is slightly unrewarding. Reading a book has a clear focus and a meaningful outcome. It is to challenge the way that you think. It is a bit like the exercise regime that includes the weekly jogs and thinking, 'I will not stop for that walk, I'm going to do the full run.' (This should not involve hands on knees halfway through.) The feeling of finishing a book still has that sense of accomplishment. You have given time, energy, and thinking to completing it, from cover to cover.

Although we are now drawn to reading more bite-sized content such as tweets and shorter articles, you can discover your creative side better by immersing yourself in a book and picking out sections to which you can bring your own slant.

GET WRITING (BUT HOW MUCH?)

Producing content for your blog should never be about frequency, but how the information is shared within your community and building an audience. Continuous content is not about creating articles five days a week. What matters is creating content that encourages an audience to build a dialogue (and also prompts the search engines to be on your side).

What happens when the 'pen' runs dry and those flashes of content inspiration become even more sporadic? It is easy to give up because no one signed up to your blog, the week got busy, or you just ran out of steam. So, you may ask yourself, 'How often should I write?' This is a mindset of consistency, not frequency. It is about deciding how often you want to/are able to write and sticking to this. Your audience needs to know what they will receive from you and when – so only commit to what is achievable. Make sure that you deliver consistently otherwise you can appear to be lacking in direction.

However, success is not just dependent on producing continuous content, but also how the content is marketed. To get results, you need to be in for the long term.

Always ask yourself, 'How am I marketing my content?' Before you dust yourself down and get back in the saddle to produce more information, understand how you are going to market it and share.

Here are some routes to consider for the longevity of your content and why marketing your content is imperative:

- **Search engine optimisation (SEO).** Content and SEO go hand in hand, but the aim is to now write for our audiences, not the search engines (and cram every keyword related to your business in one article).

- **Social media marketing.** Share your content on the various channels and link to your articles, but always remember to write differently for each channel, i.e. a paragraph cut-and-pasted from Facebook will not work on Twitter due to the 140 characters cut-off.

- **Guest blogging.** There is a host of sites that accept well-written guest blogs, and if your style of writing is accepted, it can become easy to build an audience on another platform.

- **News stories.** The world of PR still has a key role to play.

The local press is essentially relying on businesses to become journalists and produce interesting content. If you have a topic that is worthy of representing your industry, then share it.

- **Webmails.** Mailchimp provides a great way of structuring content and share what is happening within your world. For those articles that you forgot about from a month or so ago, there is an audience which is ready to interact.

- **e-books.** Articles you have produced over a number of months that relate to a specific topic can be collated and then shared with your audience as a 'best practice guide'. Also, remember there are spaces such as slideshare.net to distribute.

- **Newsletters.** Similar to e-books, if you have a collection of articles that provide a platform to build a dialogue, use it. Content needs to be 80% related to your industry and 20% related to your business. We now have the ability to become the publishers, creators, and distributors of our own information.

Audiences can be targeted through a number of platforms to ensure they empathize with your beliefs.

WATCH WHAT YOU WRITE

There is nothing worse than when someone else highlights your poor grammar. You have spent time crafting your article, but the one thing that stands out to other people is a page full of spelling and grammar mistakes. Although the spell check should be the first thing you do when you have completed your work, do not let a sloppy approach undermine your efforts and affect your credibility. The flow you create has to have pace, but also be readable.

SHARING AND PROMOTING

Too many people create an article and then write 'read my latest blog' on all social channels. What a complete waste of time. Instead, try to appreciate what will make a person click to read an article – it certainly will not be a 'read me' plea.

Do not be too self-promotional, but think of a short headline that is relevant for your audience. It could be a case study highlighting an approach that is outdated but many businesses still use, or it could be an example of something that went wrong for you, that you learned from. Promote your articles in a human way that reaches out to others where people can associate with what you write and your approach. The question you always need to ask yourself when committing to your blog is 'What value am I creating for my audience?'

ANALYTICS

One way to measure the success of your efforts and to recognize that your content strikes a chord with an audience is to run Google Analytics alongside your blog. Over time, you can see how your voice resonates with an audience and what type of article proves more popular. I found out, within a short space of time, that the articles that have a more human approach and brought in examples from my life and the problems I have faced, resulted in more views than the articles that explained generic brand thesis (I guess because these are paths taken by many others).

Please do not think that having the measurability of analytics alongside what you create is a daunting task. Treat it as a thermometer that judges how hot the content you create gets or how cold it goes to enable you to address it and to make it better. A bit of keyword analysis does not go amiss either; it is always important to understand what people are searching for. I do not want to go too in-depth here, but remember that the reason for creating content is for humans to consume it and not purely for search engines.

BE CONSISTENT

It was former British Prime Minister Benjamin Disraeli who said, 'The secret of success is consistency of purpose.'

People need to be made aware of what you represent. Make it clear that you are committed and conscientious in all your efforts so they are able to understand what your company does and what you want to be remembered for. This can be a long and sometimes lonely journey where you will ask yourself, 'Is anyone visiting, let alone reading these articles?' When you believe in the point of view that you have, and consistently portray these values, people will gradually come to recognize what you believe in. We do not need more people who talk about the same theories. What we want are people we can associate with. In other words:

RECOGNITION + FAMILIARITY = TRUST

USE IMAGERY

It can become too easy to find a clichéd image from a stock library and think that the picture of the fish jumping from a small bowl to a large bowl, or the two people shaking hands to death, will add context to your articles. This type of imagery has been done. Today, we all now have production studios in our pockets (according to CC Chapman coauthor of *The Content Rules*). Our mobiles are now at a level of which they have never been before, so why not use them to their full capability.

With the introduction of sites such as Canva, the ability to design has been opened up to everyone. The ease of creating blog graphics that can be present within your article or as an image with a tweet linking the post, has brought about a whole new world to being creative. We do not necessarily need to be trawling through Flickr or Shutterstock for our article imagery. Use your own imagination and create something that is unique to you that no one else can replicate.

KEEP WITH IT

The long-term benefit your blog provides is that your audience knows you are talking to them. You do this by reading and learning about the industry of which you are part. Over time, you will love the work that you create and find a flow to how you present yourself and the persona you've created. There is never a better feeling than when someone else acknowledges your work; it could be something as small as a retweet. The opportunity to reach out to audiences of which you may not be aware (by someone else sharing what you have produced) presents a huge opportunity for a committed and persistent mindset.

WORK TO AN EDITORIAL CALENDAR

Without going overboard, an editorial calendar is a valuable publishing schedule. Alongside commitment, there also needs to be an element of planning ahead. You need to make sure this is an ongoing process, rather than an intermittent campaign. Your blogging journey has to have a strategic focus and working to a schedule can go a long way: write for an audience, connect with your audience; exercise your mind muscle to be two weeks ahead of you; integrate messages across different channels; and become the valuable resource for your audience.

Ideas and thoughts should come from different directions and places and you should not simply sit in front of a screen waiting for the strike of inspiration to occur (trust me, it never happens). Collating thoughts helps to build up a resource of topics and personal opinion (the power of Evernote as a tool to use is fantastic) as well as encouraging your own creativity to be nurtured and flow. This helps to build your editorial calendar and create dates for publishing.

To help you with this, the WordPress Editorial Calendar plug-in can become a very useful companion, alongside some strong SEO foundations within the Yoast plug-in. Although these are not tools for cutting corners, these can encourage your strategic content focus, thinking, and behaviour.

A flat-cap story related to blogging and content creation

A few months ago, I was bought something that could either be considered quite cool, or more often than not, sign of age. I am now the proud owner of a flat cap.

I was slightly reticent in wearing it at first because adorning any form of hat has been something that I've never really done. When I first stepped out to the newsagent on a Saturday morning wearing it for the first time, I was laughed at by a couple of teenagers. Not the best start to 'wearing it in' and achieving buy-in from others.

Nevertheless, the laughing did not make me turn around, find the nearest bin, and run home in despair. I kept with it, held my head high, and rather than looking for acceptance from everyone, just persevered. I now realize that I do not want to move to the next stage and grow a moustache, I'm happy with how I am and the 'accessory' attracts comments from friends in a more positive light not just pointing and laughing.

This links (trust me here) with starting to blog and finding a place that you can call your own by creating and publishing content on a consistent basis. We all have to begin somewhere and that means doing something with which you're not necessarily familiar.

When we begin our journeys, we do not always receive the positive reinforcement we initially hoped for. Invariably, we are in a long, dark tunnel and on our own. When the content produced represents our personalities and what we believe in, we become accepted. We are acknowledged by those we wish to serve and who want to get to know us better (or already know us well enough and just reinforce what we stand for).

Now that I wear my flat cap on a more regular basis, I realize I'm not looking for social acceptance, I'm wearing this because I now feel relaxed wearing it. This is similar to the way that you write. It needs to be a reflection of the way that you speak (friendly and approachable) and above all else, being human and not regurgitate industry jargon.

To gain positive reinforcement, we have to be in it for the long haul. We cannot set foot outside of our house for the first time wearing something a bit different and become regarded as slick by the rest of the world. Acceptance takes time, and if we are looking to build an audience who believes in us, we have to be committed and consistent. This is intended to generate momentum in the way that others see us and how we want to be perceived (and taken seriously).

Coming back to the hat, I'm now wearing it more frequently. Although wearing a cap is not for everyone, neither is blogging. It is just something that you need to throw yourself into and keep with if you want to showcase who you are and your point of view.

YOUR EMAIL

There is nothing new or revolutionary about email; it is tried and tested. The word email was coined back in the early 1990s (but the origins of a digital message service has its roots in the 1960s). The role it plays for businesses today is still a key tool to help build your digital space and own it. There are now more than 3.2 billion email accounts worldwide and the number is expected to rise to more than 4.9 billion by 2017 (according to a study from the Radicati Group).

Although we all get to grips with the social channels with which we feel most comfortable, email still provides us with the greatest opportunity to have a dialogue with an audience. We would all agree that email is reliable, easy to use, and straightforward to control.

The world of social media is becoming more and more about building a digital persona (how we want others to see us), rather than creating an authentic voice. I have mentioned before how tiresome it can be reading on social channels how busy people are, with the aim of coming across as important. Email lets us stamp our own personality on what we write and we can get to understand what works for our audience and ourselves. Email allows us to be intimate and personal and this can be the catalyst to help build relationships. The ability for email to connect on a one-to-one level can help support two-way communication. Although the world of social media is about shared conversation, one of the greatest strengths of email is the ability to bring the dialogue to a more personal space and target exactly who you want.

Social media works within your own digital space is where the social media connections can then be moved over to what is yours (by asking permission of the person with whom you are in contact; naturally we cannot move Twitter accounts to our email). This is where you are in control of the experience and whether it is to build a stronger direct conversation or to add to your database, you are in the driving seat. Email marketing relationships have such an important role to play. You own the message, when it is sent, to whom it is sent, and the ongoing dialogue.

When we consider Facebook/Twitter/LinkedIn/Google+ a main source of information and not just a distribution channel, we forfeit any intellectual property rights we thought we had. When we create and build platforms over which we have complete control, it becomes far easier to let a relationship develop and have an audience which understands what you believe in and the relevant, useful, and entertaining content you produce.

To build your audience, the one thing over which you need to have control, is the ability to grow and nurture your database.

BUILD YOUR DATABASE

The simplest way to define the importance of building a database is that it is free; it is valuable and can assist in building your customer base. If you have an ongoing commitment to growing and monitoring your database, it becomes such a valuable marketing tool.

Here is why it is vital to focus on your database:

- **It is simple to set up** The easiest method is to set up a database via Excel. It is not a sophisticated tool, but can produce results when used correctly. For instance, transferring Excel to an online software format is a simple process.
- **It is a catalyst for growth** The information you collate (by asking other businesses you meet whether it is OK to 'add you to our database' and gaining their permission) helps capture potential customers.
- **It can turn prospects into customers** If you can build a dialogue and be visible in what you do and keep people informed, this is so much more effective than sitting quietly and no-one knowing how you can help.
- **It can help formulate campaigns** According to Jay Levinson (author of *Guerrilla Marketing*), the science of using databases for direct mail follows a 60-30-10 rule. Levinson states: '60% is based on having the right list of people; 30% depends on you making the right offer; 10% depends on the creative package.'

- **Optimize your networking methods** Nothing is better than complementing your networking connections by utilizing your database as a follow-on and keeping a dialogue continuous.

- **A good way of measuring your campaigns** Using your database and targeting via campaigns lets you monitor and determine the level of success. Moving from product-based messages to content-driven information, can change the dynamic for your business.

Utilizing a database means that customers and prospects who have 'opted in' are open to receiving the information you send. Make sure the opportunity for people to sign up to your database is prominent throughout your website. If you are going to make sure you stay in contact on a regular basis, stick to it. You need people to sign up based on the useful information that will make their businesses better. You need to be more sophisticated than the 'subscribe to our email list' and consider ways that add value such as 'receive emails every Wednesday on a topic in which you specialize'.

One of the biggest things to remember with an email database is that it is not about the size and pursuit of collecting numbers; it is about the quality of the audience (there is nothing worse than handing someone your business card and a week later you're receiving emails to which you did not subscribe). The only thing that matters is that your audience is engaged with the content you produce and the products and services you deliver. It is better to have a small database of people who interact and participate, than a huge database of people who are not interested.

With the of mobile devices, it is now vital to consider how well your email message renders on mobile. According to research by Pure360 (based on 35,000 different emails sent by more than 119 companies in 23 sectors), 28% of emails are opened on mobile devices, but only

10% lead to clicks. This highlights the importance of the role that mobile plays for today's businesses.

Building a database and targeting an audience is not about the pursuit of collecting numbers; what matters is how we define others as people. The way we connect with others is the crux for all content to be a success and to build an audience who warms to us and is willing to engage with what we believe in. Email is the best way to define an actual audience as real people.

THE TYPES OF EMAIL THAT WORK FOR YOUR AUDIENCE

Emails serve a number of purposes: maintaining a dialogue, highlighting the problems you solve, and encouraging the sales process. Utilising your email is the most cost-effective way to distribute a message to an audience and to maintain a process of keeping in touch with your database.

A prospect needs to warm to you, understand your point of view, and build a positive perception before a dialogue moves to a profitable outcome. Keeping in contact in a number of ways where your subscribers understand how useful you are, can result in the reward you are looking for.

E-NEWSLETTER

Within the world of content marketing, the e-newsletter is a valuable piece of armoury to encourage interaction, draw an audience to a particular area of your website, and generate a call to action. With the development of sites such as Mailchimp that now encourage creativity and developing ideas, creating and distributing e-newsletters has never been more accessible. The secret to a successful newsletter is to maintain a commitment as an ongoing activity to your communications plan.

E-BOOKS AND RESOURCES WITH A LONGER SHELF-LIFE

Demonstrating your expertise and knowledge (for example via the creation of e-books and resources that have involved an amount of time to produce) has longevity. Target your database and treat them as a VIP group which has the first opportunity to view and download, before content is released to a wider audience. This does not mean a link to a Slideshare presentation, but something that is located within your source (your website or blog).

ACKNOWLEDGMENT

Even from the first touch point, be thankful for someone's commitment. This could be a prospect subscribing to your e-newsletter or blog. A personal email to thank them for taking time to come to your side and listen to your viewpoint involves a very personal interaction. This is in the opposite direction from a generic 'thank you for subscribing, now like us on Facebook' in the inbox.

We need to become more interactive with an audience which has made that commitment. We need to acknowledge members. The world has become far too automated, so let's become more present. When a person signs up to your webinar, ebook or event why not take the time to get in touch with a personal message.

Co-author of *The Rebel's Guide To Email Marketing*, DJ Waldow, highlights that businesses need to become more personable when it comes to email marketing. The biggest mistake that businesses make is:

'BLASTING. Just like any other marketing channel, you have to respect your audience. If you are blasting emails to your subscribers, it implies you have not targeted the messaging to be timely, relevant, and valuable to them. There is nothing worse then getting a message that from a marketer that annoys you. Email - when done right - should be more like a conversation: engaging, useful, fun, valuable, human.'

ENSURING YOUR EMAILS ARE OPENED (WHAT NOT TO DO)

It is easy to sit back and think that the email message that you have crafted is worthy of a response and gratitude, but there can be many reasons your emails are not opened. It's easy to get excited with open rates between 20% and 30%, but when it hits a very small percentage, there is a reason. Let's have a brief look at the surefire way to lose any momentum you were hoping to build.

The subject heading is not compelling

The 'hurry up, offer ends today'-type message does not work anymore. With the constant mix of work-related requests, updates, and sales messages, most people scan through what is awaiting them and delete what is not relevant. It is no wonder that open rates are pretty low with generic headings that strike no chord with a recipient. According to salesforce.com, 33% of email recipients open emails based on subject line alone.

The subject heading is the equivalent of a paragraph

Keeping the email subject line limited to a short sentence negates the need to spell out the entirety of the message. The only thing in which the recipient is interested at a glance is 'What's in it for me?' Remember that many emails are now opened on mobile devices and if the subject lines are too long, they will not be visible and cut off mid-sentence.

You're not relevant

If you receive an email from someone of whom you are not aware, that email is almost instantly put in the 'trash'. The name that is visible onscreen is the first thing a recipient will see (also sending an email from info@ or enquiries@ is asking for it to be deleted as there is no human element to these messages – see the next point). Being unfamiliar instinctively raises suspicion and rings alarm bells, along with 'Where did they get my address from?' or 'Did I sign up for this?' responses. According to research by Return Path, the average subscriber receives 416 commercial emails a month.

You're not humanising

From the subject line to your opening intro, you need others to see that you are a real person looking to engage. You should never start with 'Dear Sir/Madam' or a personal favourite, 'Dear potential customer', where the whole activity is based on sending the same email to everyone on a list. If you're looking to build that introduction, as with any stage of the sales process, you need to know more about the prospect (at least their name). Even if that means a bit of research to find out more about the person with whom you are looking to target, it can be a far more rewarding experience. To make an impression you need to be more specific to the person you're looking to build a one-to-one dialogue with, rather than using words such as 'free', 'one-off', or 'exclusive offer' in the subject heading.

You're not measuring and learning

The biggest lesson I learned when emailing messages from a database was to monitor the success of each campaign. The most wasteful thing you can do is to distribute an email, have a sense of release that you pressed the send button, and then move on to the next job. When my company first started to use email as a method of communicating with an audience, we were sporadic and the content was more product led than education-based. As measuring techniques became more readily available, to check click through rates, the times of the day when emails were opened, and which people from the database were becoming allies, patterns started emerging. One of the biggest strengths in using email is that you have the ability to target an audience and learn how it works. Tune into your results and make sure you do not do your brand and yourself a disservice. From my own experience, when sending our 'You Are The Media' news digest, the articles that resulted in higher open rates are those articles that have a story that others can relate to. For instance, a customer had entered a national award and had beaten an exhibition at the Victoria and Albert museum (in London) for David Bowie, so naturally the headline focused on the company beating a world-renowned musician.

THE REASON YOUR CONTENT EFFORTS WILL FAIL

The reason content marketing fails for many businesses has nothing to do with articles that no one reads, emails that are left bold in the inbox, and websites that do not stand for something. It's simpler than that.

In the words of Leonardo Da Vinci, 'Art is never finished, only abandoned.' Let's take out the word 'art' and replace it with 'content' and we are getting closer to the truth. As your business adopts a mindset that is more about an ongoing commitment rather than a campaign mentality, there is still a mythical belief that if you create content and distribute via LinkedIn or Twitter with a link to a related article to your website, then the next step is someone will click on the 'contact us' page and the sale is 80% done. Based on the strength of one blog post, a PDF download, or the first e-newsletter that is sent to a prospect.

The biggest discipline I have found when any business looks to adopt a content marketing approach is patience and persistence. As someone who specializes in communications, you can no longer produce a series of adverts or the company brochure in isolation to build trust and resonance. Content must be grounded in consistency.

It can be an isolating journey, but you have to start somewhere. Instead of dabbling with many social channels, try to commit to just a few and be consistent. I was close to putting my blog to one side at the end of 2012 as I believed that no-one was listening (or rather reading) and the time spent on writing articles was becoming a fruitless task. The reason I decided to stick with the journey is that

I guest-posted on other blog sites and started seeing the number of visitors to my site increase as a result. Where at first the subscribers to the blog were people from within my immediate circle (or rather people who were more friends than business associates), I started seeing email addresses from people with whom I had no relationship (and not an odd-reading Gmail/Yahoo spam address). Slowly, more people were willing to find out more about me and what I had to say.

To start to build resonance, you need a purpose to become more human (by engaging with others). I originally thought that the end result of writing blog posts and sharing information was others consuming content and as a conversion tool to encourage them to buy. I now see the purpose is to target a niche audience with articles and downloads to encourage them to stand for something too. If they are looking for a helping hand for their business, they know where to come. A more valuable and loyal customer is built from someone who sees you as a valuable resource and you become their first port of call when they are looking for specific advice and business support.

In being consistent, we want others to make an association and to build a rapport with our businesses. Consistency is only built by having a structure in place. If structure is created from a source (your website) and then distributed (via the social channels with which you're comfortable), this can become your key indicator that you are progressing on the right path. Let's not forget to also embrace email as an old friend in the consistency process.

Being consistent, means being present. As author, speaker, and marketer Chris Brogan highlighted in one of his Sunday email newsletters (this is highly recommended), to 'get better at something, you need to do it daily'. He even created a formula for the process:

SPECIFICITY + FREQUENT PRACTICE = SUCCESS

SEO rankings and industry credibility will never be built from dabbling intermittently in content marketing. The nirvana never originated from the one PowerPoint presentation you created that is now present on Slideshare. It is similar to the lawn that I'm trying to grow at the moment.

From the seed that was originally spread onto the lawn, I'm now realizing it is not a case of throwing the empty grass seed bag away and then waiting for the results. You have to tend to the lawn to make sure the grass grows across a consistent area and is not a patchy mess. You have to show a level of commitment to a process that you need to repeat over time and accept that the fully-grown lawn may not necessarily be ready for the barbeque within a couple of months. We have to accept that to achieve the best results, you need a longer-term mindset. To be meaningful, you cannot give up.

The one thing you cannot do is stop. Patience, persistence, and perseverance are the key attributes a business needs to make their content marketing efforts a success. The biggest mistake many businesses make is that they give up on their content efforts way to soon. It is a marathon that we are running, not a sprint; let's enjoy getting fitter and being prepared. In the words of Seth Godin, we have to "want the wanting".

LET'S ROUND OFF AND SAY GOODBYE TO THE TOOLS THAT DO NOT WORK ANYMORE

When your marketing is in the wrong hands, it can become a costly and wasteful experience.

In summary, we need to stop trying to solve problems via the communication methods that were pertinent 10 years ago. The issues on the table today are totally different from the ones that were here a decade ago.

We need to learn to move away from the old-school 'tools of the trade': product-based messages; ego-driven, self-congratulatory website pages; a return on advertising, which does not justify the expenditure; and local press business pages cutting and pasting 'me-too' press releases.

It is lazy and irresponsible for marketers to settle for the way that brand exposure and persuasion has always been. It is bad practice to resort to tactics that are now out of kilter with the way that business (and society) behaves. It is a bit like a parent buying their child a Tamagotchi for their birthday and saying that people still play with them. I noticed things had to change for my business when the person who was responsible for sales treated everyone with whom they spoke exactly the same. Every business with which the salesperson had a conversation was driven by what he thought the prospect should be reacting to, i.e. two or three heavy sales calls and then the expectation of a sale. This is the polar opposite of recognising that building any form of relationship takes time. It requires an understanding of the prospect, their market, and what makes them tick.

I am proud to say that recognizing what is right and wrong for my business has now led to a total change and approach. It has now moved to creating relevant information for a marketplace to become more informed. All businesses need to understand that building engagement takes time and the imaginary 'buy before next Friday' message will not work. Many businesses still use this as an angle of attack to throw their sales messages to every business in the hope of gaining some form of attention and reaction.

THE FAILED MARKETING LIST OF SHAME
We can no longer build our businesses on expectation and what has been historically accepted as the way to brand. Without getting carried away, if any of these from the list of shame are a key feature in your current marketing activity, it is time to sit and reflect on your current practices (but it is ok, there is a solution):

- **Relying on the 'subscribe to our newsletter'** prompt on your homepage or even better when the word '*FREE*' is included (whenever did a newsletter have monetary value?).

- **Keyword stuffing** to gain an SEO promise of recognition by cramming in words that are relevant to your business. This will lead to you being recognized for the wrong reasons.

- **Repeating the same message on every social channel**. By syncing your Facebook updates with your Twitter account, Facebook posts read as complete nonsense. It only takes a few minutes to tailor your message for each channel you use.

- **Press advertising to boast how good you are**. You cannot dictate a message to an audience that focuses 100% on product benefits and not the reason why your product or service solves problems for others. If you do this, then the customer becomes almost irrelevant and not the focus of your content.

- **Flat PR messages that are used to brag.** By accepting that the way for others to buy into you is sharing a bland press release based on: Your efforts to work with a charity in the local area; entering an award and making it to the final (before the winner is announced); or the new account executive. Be aware that these methods are outdated.

- **Website content focused on how good your business is.** No one is bothered about why you offer the best customer service and why your staff live and breathe the company ethos. The 'about us' page has become stuffed with corporate hot air and is the equivalent of being at a networking event and someone taking to the centre of the room and asking 'hands up who likes me'.

- **Purchasing a database of strangers' details**. You cannot think that this will help you to build a rapport after one email is sent and then be disappointed when you do not get an immediate return. We cannot rely on other companies to deliver our message to people who have no idea who we are. This is the equivalent of trying to get a stranger to open the door and buy from us.

- **Websites regurgitating printed sales material.** It can become far too easy for one piece of communication to be a carbon copy of another, regardless of how your audience prefers to consume its preferred type of media. The overt sales message from the brochure becoming a cut-and-paste effort for a website shows a lack of creativity or appreciation of an audience which is willing to build a conversation.

THE SOLUTION TO TAKE FORWARD

The key message here is to remember that for people to buy from you, they have to buy into you as a business and what you stand for. People buy into the approach you provide to help solve their problems. Content is not king; it's the driving force behind engaging with others via the media channel that they prefer to consume.

I'm not saying that traditional media has had its day, namely print and advertising. It is just that the conversation has shifted to a multitude of places. This has been brought on by the social empowerment of the web plus the traditional distribution of media now being democratized. This allows anyone to create, curate, and distribute to the audiences that they target, build, and control. There is a whole world of information overload of which we are all part, which has been created by us. The answer is not about creating more: press releases, more PDF downloads, daily blog articles, greater presence on Twitter, more landing pages. The solution is found in grabbing the attention of our audience in the places where they are aware of us and keeping momentum with compelling and engaging content.

The challenge for businesses is not to put the focus on sharing the 'contact us' page on every message as a sign-off, but for you to:

- Become focused on a target audience (and positioned as the logical choice)

- Change from being transactional to becoming more conversational

- Invite customers to become more involved in the solutions for others

- Commit to an ongoing conversation

- Only utilize traditional methods (such as printed newsletters,) with an audience who know you and will be receptive to it

- Create a passionate point of view

- Aggregate your own audience rather than thinking that buying a database is the answer

- Produce consistent quality, not sporadic distraction

- Understand that relationships require nurturing and take time to develop

- Be present. Automation is horrible: do not 'broadcast' when you are not actually there

What can work for you is to channel the stories and messages via a source (the company website), accompanied by the blog and email. Then, by using distribution channels (social media), you can encourage exchange and bring conversation to the places where you have ownership (your website, blog, and email).

Burying your head in the sand believing that you can persist with yesterday's marketing tools is doomed to failure. You have many ways engaging, connecting, sharing, and growing. It is up to you to use the channels and platforms you have inherited both responsively and carefully.

CHAPTER 8

SERVING OTHERS

Your journey has to be centred on changing your mindset and approaching the world of marketing differently from the masses. Let's now look at how a more generous approach can help to solidify a credible brand built on trust, authenticity, and honesty. What I mean by being 'generous' is committing to supporting other businesses or people within your wider community (I do not mean just those local to you, but those within your audience). To be generous, you need to genuinely care about the businesses and people with whom you engage and show that you understand what they stand for. It is only when they feel this level of support from you that you will be able to develop relationships that work on a deeper level.

Let's get straight to the point: no one is bothered about how much you profess to know or how good your business is. What matters is that you care beyond collecting money.

Influencers have always been present. What is different today is that the social web means that anyone can self-claim to be an 'expert' to a wider audience purely by promoting what they do. This is a soulless tactic to pursue.

If you think of this within the context of supporters for a football team: 99% of a filled football stadium comprises people that are sure they know the right tactics to play, the team that should be starting, and what is going wrong with the current season, but how would they really fare as the manager?

Looking deeper and at social profiles, we are awash with self-confessed 'ninjas', 'rock stars', and 'speakers' who spew forth articles that are repeated from other places. They believe that what they are professing is true, and are sharing what they think should be shared (because it is the same thing that others have said before them). The question is, does the audience really care?

The moment someone cares is when they see that you have an obligation to serve others within your marketplace and community. When you have carved your space and others begin to recognize your approach is one of generosity – then things will start to change for your business. When you care about others, the selling aspect becomes easier and the ability to build an audience becomes more accessible.

According to Edelman Insights, *Consumer Marketing Survey*, customers place a high importance on brands giving back to the community. A total of 90% of respondents said they wanted brands to share and only 10% believed that brands do it well. This provides a huge opportunity for businesses to take on a way of operating that is focused on sharing our passions and beliefs, rather than taking from the communities that we serve.

Earlier in this book, I mentioned the importance of providing content for free. A generous attitude can go beyond what you create. It is a mindset that your business embraces and at its core is the acknowledgment of the emotional attachment you have with an audience by becoming believable, responsible, and purposeful to others.

BECOMING BELIEVABLE TO OTHERS

The messages we deliver to our audiences have to be believable to our overall story.

Authenticity is a key factor in a business being accepted. Everything that we stand behind has to be convincing for others to understand, so that others can see that we represent a trusted and credible brand. It is easier than ever to self-proclaim that we are experts in our marketplace and then promote that our businesses have a responsibility for the communities of which we are part. Eventually, it comes across as an empty promise filled with PR helium. As businesses, we need to create the whole package rather than standing to the side and observing what everyone else is doing. To do this, you need to be clear in your own thinking. Ask yourself, 'What does my business stand for that is different from other businesses within the same marketplace?' and 'What do I truly believe in?/What is my vision for this business/industry?' Once you have this in mind, it is much easier to be authentic and create a consistent voice in line with this.

The case for transparency and track record is becoming more apparent. This is something that Innocent Drinks promises where 10% of business profits are given to charity. Its *Tastes good does good* campaign shifted from the product benefits to a more emotional message on the community work that the company delivers. The Innocent foundation was set up to make a stance to assist the world's hungry and projects have been initiated in 20 countries, focusing on 'supporting people dependent on subsistence agriculture' (according to Innocent's sustainable legacy). This showcases a company that puts others first, including Innocent's support for UK Charity 'FareShare', to redistribute food and drink to those who need it most. Innocent has a long-term view focused on thinking about others and then sharing that passion and belief. This also applies to the mindset and delivery for small businesses.

As business leaders, we need to live and breathe what we do and the benefits we can provide other people. It is worthless to treat what we do as 'a job'. For others to buy in, we have to understand deeply their perspective. It has been a tough few years for all of us, but we still have to support the spaces we represent and deliver tangible and emotional value to others. It is pointless declaring on Twitter that you are proud to support an initiative when all it represents is a short-term goal to an overall PR initiative. People now want to see evidence of your continued commitment. It is only when you provide this that you will be seen as a credible business that gives back and has ethics.

Sometimes we need a fresh perspective to see what we are doing. We can believe that we represent an authentic message, but underneath the surface the same pair of eyes still sees the same flaws, day in, day out.

Here are six ways to create believable brands:

- Create experiences that cannot be associated with another product or service

- Deliver a brand that stands for something

- Create value and deliver it consistently

- Be honest and truthful about what your business does for others and how you do this

- Learn to become more social and not hide behind a digital persona

- Become relevant to others to encourage engagement

The messages you create and distribute need to be believable and relate to the experience you have, rather than the product or service you sell. Although the majority of businesses still sit within their product-driven worlds, why not champion the authentic brand you represent and believe in?

YOUR BIGGEST INVESTMENT

To accomplish what you want to achieve and to become recognized for it, you need to invest time.

My wife is a brilliant cook who will spend time perfecting a recipe, until she is happy. Although I am more than happy with toad in the hole, her ventures into dishes from around the world involve time and effort in making sure she is happy with how everything comes together and is presented.

We have to be patient to allow the correct cooking times to produce an end result that reflects all the time and effort that has been put into it. With cooking, you cannot cut corners or miss an ingredient. If you do, it can affect the taste or how everything finally looks. There are two options when it comes to cooking: we can pay someone else to do the job for us (namely phoning one of the restaurants in town to deliver) or if the time is taken to outdo the restaurant, it becomes a more rewarding and fulfilling experience.

When you put this into a business context, if you look to grow your skill-sets and areas of knowledge you can become more competent in (and I'm not saying here that buying the latest 4K camera makes you a videographer or learning InDesign from scratch makes you a designer; that takes years of learning). With passion, interest, and commitment, you can look to grow your knowledge and delivery.

It is not the best route to take a 'hired gun' approach to look after social media. We have to be present and 'in the now' to respond, communicate, and engage with people, not employ other people to pretend to be us. The reality of everything is that to be good at something can take a lot of time. With the platforms and channels that are freely available to us, time to become more accomplished is our biggest investment. The world is now a relatively level playing field. With enthusiasm and dedication to learn continually, we can strive to be better at something than the competition.

GENEROSITY IS THE NEXT STEP AFTER 'ADDED VALUE'

Although the world now rewards generosity, there are many businesses (including mine a couple of years ago) that believe we have to be insular and to keep our best work to ourselves. Why should we show others how things need to be done; this is what customers need to pay for, right? To some it may almost feel like opening the magic box and showing all the tricks that are used to give someone else competitive advantage.

People who believe that sharing leads to other people stealing ideas and business are naive. A self-centred mindset believes that if you aim to inform and help others, then potential customers are going to think they can replicate what you provide, rather than thinking that eventually someone will not be able to do it themselves and at that point whom will they turn to?

A mindset that is self-focused follows Scrooge's belief that Christmas is a 'time for finding yourself older and not an hour richer'. Rather than holding things back, there is great reward in releasing. Instead, try to develop a mindset of continuous value. For instance, it is far easier to play by the new rules and have a focus on solving problems from a customer's perspective and add value. If a self-centred mindset promotes insecurity, then one of generosity understands the need for you and how your help will never go away.

The more generous you are, the more you stay true to yourself. In the words of ethnologist Richard Dawkins, 'Let us try to teach generosity and altruism, because we are born selfish.' We cannot let the way that things have been done before constrain us. Instead, adopt an authentic, honest and 'useful to others' mindset.

BEING OPEN WITH OTHERS

When content marketing works, it is because the focus is on creating stories/information/perspectives that are worth talking about and sharing. Let's be a bit more specific: today, marketing is about creating useful interaction around human experiences. What becomes a common wrong for businesses is when it comes to the creation of content centred on the bestowing of knowledge by directly telling people what to do.

I have previously highlighted how important it is to be seen as an 'educator'. However, before we take to the front of the classroom with the light pen gesticulating and punching our fists at passionate beliefs, after watching *Dead Poets Society*, I believe we should get to know ourselves a bit better first. Many businesses have effectively graduated to an educational role before they have done the groundwork. To be a successful educator, we must ensure we understand what the role means – it's not to tell people how to behave with lists of 'must haves', 'how-tos', and 'reasons'.

Businesses can all too easily create content that tells people how to behave, then sit idly waiting for customers to come to them (and wondering why they do not!).

Putting this belief into everyday terms, it is a bit like the relationship with my neighbour. When it comes to DIY and manly expectations, I think I am devoid of testosterone. I have struggled and given up on many projects such as the garden shed I tried to assemble and the garden table I have attempted to construct. However, my neighbour has always been ready to give advice over the fence on what I have been doing wrong, what I need to do, or acknowledge that I am making a shambles of what I have taken on. There has always been this barrier between us, ie the fence, and it is all too easy to comment on what I am doing wrong, when actually what I need is helpful advice (or better yet, for him to come and show me!).

This is what is happening within the social web, particularly from our original sources (our websites and our blogs). We have the virtual fence that businesses are looking over and saying the equivalent of 'Here are 10 ways you should be putting that paint on.' The problem is that businesses do not acknowledge how they have faced the problems themselves, taken a step back to be better, figure out what was not working, and share their knowledge in a way that is believable, in their own voice, with humility and authenticity.

In studies, the majority of people overestimate their IQ, according to psychologist David Dunning. For instance, in a classic study from 1977, 94% of professors rated themselves above average when related to their peers. The study also found that people overestimate how charitable they will be towards future donation causes, but accurately guess their peers' donation traits.

If we are now getting specific, the term this relates to is 'illusory superiority', which is defined as 'people overestimate their positive qualities and underestimate their negative traits.' In business, our aim is to stand out from the competition, sell to an audience, and drive profitability, but the 'above average effect' is prevalent for many businesses that create content and tell others how to do their job better. Going back to the concept of becoming a teacher – the ones who were most effective were those who, instead of telling us what to do, acknowledged a problem, deconstructed it, and then shared how the problem was solved. This is what we as businesses need to do for one another.

Let's not ignore our failures. The ability to learn from them is as important as sharing how we found a resolution. Generosity leads to trust and if we care and persist by acknowledging that we all face problems that need to be tackled, then we are in the business of connecting. There is nothing wrong with highlighting what we have done wrong and how we have learned from this and made our businesses stronger. Let's put the 'I talk, you listen' mentality to one side. The most valuable thing we can do is to create experiences that other people (and businesses) share and take on board. To be seen as successful, we need to contribute our perspective to an audience who is ready to stick by us and leave the gate open for those who are not interested to exit.

We need to create a community that shares our involvement with the real world and help guide others to ask the right questions about their own business, so they can find the answers for themselves. This goes right back to the days of the caveman. No one stood in front of a group of hairy people and said '*here are ten ways how you should light a fire.*' The first person who ever managed to light a fire succeeded by trying and failing many times. Once they had achieved this, they were then able to pass on to others what they had learnt.

Persistently telling other people what to do is an empty tactic in an ocean of noise. Many businesses are happy to clamour for people's attention, every minute of the day. However, the answer to gaining attention is to become better at educating and supporting others so they can find the solution for themselves. To build your level of trust as an influencer and not a self-proclaimed expert is a route that provides real reward.

We need to change our core set of beliefs from disrupting, self-importance, and product promotion. The future is about becoming more open with sharing our experiences from the world around us that have particular relevance to the marketplaces within which we operate. Let's get better at telling our own stories. We cannot set ourselves on pedestals and tell everyone that we are better than anyone else. What we can be is real people (and businesses) that have the ability to take a step back, look at things that we consider broken, find solutions, and share these with others. If we want to be seen as honest and trustworthy, we need to share experiences that show we are.

The intention is for others to come to you as an equal and for them to seek your advice. This goes back to the days of school and the lessons in which you became totally uninterested were when the learning was dictated from an old set of principles and theory and you sat there with heavy eyes and waning attention span. The lessons that worked were when the teacher was engaging and passionate and generated interest through involving you with the learning process. Especially if they could apply the learning to the real world and draw upon their own experiences. We need to use the same principles when using social platforms and the spaces that we create. Remember that dictation and instruction of message is tiresome when it is not compelling and fails to make a connection with us.

It is time to stop telling others what to do and become more open. You need to share, within a community, your failures, your viewpoints, and also how to help others see the solutions to the problems that arise from your professional arena. This is what a generous approach is all about. It is time for you to stand up for being normal again and champion your own deficiencies, views, and understanding of the commercial world around you.

SEVEN WAYS TO EMBRACE A GENEROUS MINDSET

To become influential within your marketplace, you need to demonstrate a wider acknowledgment of the role that you play for others and within your wider community. Here are some ways to embrace an attitude that benefits others, as well as securing long-term gain for your business:

- **Educate others in your local area**
  There are many ways within your community to share what you have learned. Involvement with colleges and universities as guest lecturers can be an ongoing commitment. Involvement in initiatives such as the Young Enterprise can be a rewarding experience and you may also learn new things from the young,

savvy, and fresh individuals who will enter your marketplace in the coming years. Many businesses are quick to say how busy they are or how good their year has been. Why do more people not give their time to share their experiences? Creating learning and sharing platforms for local business groups is a completely different approach that will showcase what you have learnt rather than what you have to sell.

- **Sharing your competencies**
  No-one is going to sneak up from behind and replicate your ideas. Just because you had selflessly shared with an audience what you have learned and gave pointers to other businesses to solve their problems, does not mean that everyone else will copy you. There is nothing wrong with professing how you have found solutions to people's problems. Whether this is via a blog or demonstrating via video, the media routes that you choose are yours to demonstrate how you have helped.

- **Re-educate and remould**
  We have never had a better time to relearn and push our strategic thinking to help others, whether this is by reading, listening to podcasts, and generally being aware of the world around you, President of Twist, Mitch Joel stated: 'Being inspired is not a destination. You need to get inspired and proactively look to become energized. To find my inspiration I began by reading a lot of books. If you do not know where to begin, reading widely is always a good way to start (the good news is by reading this you have already begun your journey). Reading is always accessible, from the library to any major news site. There are many places to become exhilarated. No matter how niche your business is there are always opportunities. One thing to remember is that being inspired is different from having the time, effort, energy and desire to publish. Make sure that before you begin, you have inspiration to write. Otherwise you stare at a blank screen and the screen stares blankly back.'

- **Trigger others**

  When you are regarded as a consistent source of information to your audience, you then have the essence to trigger a reaction from others and for them to stick by the point of view that you represent. Once you have a community of subscribers who trust and believe you, the opportunities to then ask for something in return becomes easier than it once was (for instance, to direct people to a piece of content that would be of interest or to a new project that may be valuable to purchase).

- **Provide evidence**

  If you are highlighting the values of using a technique, then you need to show proof from the experiences you have had. This could be a commitment to a weekly e-newsletter to your audience on a chosen day, without fail. Show people what failed and what has worked. Real-world examples that are not just regurgitating theory from textbooks will always generate a better level of engagement.

- **Stand tall at what you do**

  To be recognized as a trusted influencer in your industry, you have to care about what you do. More importantly, enjoy the role that you play within your marketplace and do not take yourself too seriously. If what you produce has a lack of focus, is not compelling enough, and lacks a clear voice, it becomes difficult to understand. Stand tall and project to others what you believe in. You now have more media channels than ever to show who you are, so take your place on the podium. Do not settle for the bronze position.

- **Be more human**

  You started your business with something in which you believed and the goal to find solutions for others. To stand out from the competition, you need to have the courage to make a more honest connection with people in a more accessible and transparent way. The secret is to let your personality come to the surface and show your warmth, even if that means showing your vulnerable side. You have got to show others that you have a soul, and that you are not a meaningless foghorn in an empty tunnel. Although we are encouraged to share our messages with as many people as possible, let's flip that and become more meaningful to those with whom we connect. This is what gives purpose to your businesses by including others and not excluding them. There is nothing wrong with starting a project that does not deliver commercial success, as long as you follow it through. We all have fears (fear of rejection, fear of a lack of gratitude, fear of being unhappy) and it is great to know that what you do does have an effect on people. Being seen by your audience members who love what you do (even if it may not be perfect) is an enriching experience in its own right.

To prove to others that you care and have a wider responsibility (other than sending out invoices), you have to be continually present. If the quest is to be popular and to focus on collecting followers on social channels, then you will not achieve acknowledgment from any audience. To become recognized as a generous provider of information and knowledge, your key ingredients are: the investment of time, making sure you are of use to others, and you are open to future learning experiences.

BIG HEART Looking For The One Who....

...is honest, can relate to, has empathy, is creative, is positive, has ambition and drive, shares the same core beliefs.

Are you the one?

CONCLUSION

The most pertinent message that I want you to take from this book is that as a business, you need to direct your energy towards building meaningful relationships with people who matter.

Technology now allows you to reach out to people whom you have never met before and in a more purposeful way. They do not have to have met you, for you to build a relationship with them. People still like to buy from people, rather than faceless brands; it is that simple. The more you can humanize your brand, the better.

When looking to build a successful relationship (whether personal or professional) there are several traits that people tend to look for, before they are willing to become loyal and committed:

Honesty: you have to show that you are trustworthy. This is the foundation of any successful relationship and just like in personal relationships, it takes time to grow. Without trust, you will never gain commitment from the consumer or develop a loyal relationship that leads to repeat business that turns a customer into an advocate. This is attained by creating a brand that is credible and that stands for something. It is also about proving that you have evidence to show that you follow these principles through in real life. You need to show that you believe in what you say by being consistent with the content that you deliver. It is important to be honest about sharing your business story with others, the mistakes you have made, and what you have learned from them. Sharing this level of knowledge will generate respect from others. Deeper trusting relationships come from the knowledge that you can reflect on and learn from your own mistakes.

Someone to relate to: relationships become solidified when you share things of interest. This generates an open discussion and helps to build reciprocal respect from both parties. Your ability to tell stories and share real-life experiences is one of the ways in which your audience will be able to relate to you as a person. Great content that is produced and delivered will always engage and communicate. The reason is that when an emotional connection is made, value is created.

Empathy: you need to show you understand your audience and can empathize with the problems they experience. This is demonstrated by your ability to solve your audience's problems and discuss topics that are relevant to them. Again, like in a personal relationship, it may take time to gain an understanding of who your audience is first before a conversation starts to flow. Your whole objective, as a business, is to create something more meaningful for your customers. For instance, a restaurant is not just a place to eat food but a place that is guilt free.

Equality: although it is important to have expertise in a particular area, portraying yourself as an 'expert' means that the relationship will never be equal. Although your audience members may come to you occasionally for advice, they may not feel like they can hold an ongoing dialogue with you. It is more important to have a collaborative and sharing mindset, where your role within your community is to help others. A big differentiator that you can provide to your marketplace is to serve your audience with intent and purpose.

Creativity: it makes sense that an audience wants to connect with people who have something new and exciting to say. Showing that you have creativity will set you apart from others and entice others to engage with you.

Relevant: people are attracted to brands that have a meaning to which they can relate. If you are relevant to enough people, you then become distinctive in the eyes of others. We have never lived in a more interesting time to be valuable to other people and to create direct relationships. The competition can copy everything that you do, but they cannot copy how you communicate in a consistent manner. Remember, this is all about people, not products.

Generosity: an audience looks to be valued and one of the ways you can show them that you care is to share your content regularly and freely. You need to be committed to remaining transparent and persisting in the business of connecting with others. This way you can show that you deliver value upfront, rather than claiming that you are the company to work with. To become generous, you need to become accessible to others via the information that is created. If you can do this with authority and warmth, then you can become a preferred choice. Plus, being generous as a person and a business makes you feel good.

Positivity: having contact with people who have a problem-solving mindset is both refreshing and inspiring. What you have to remember is that to gain attention, you have to earn it with drive and determination. Once your audience interprets your attitude, it can buy into your approach that concentrates on providing solutions.

Ambition and drive: people want someone who is committed to their cause and has the right attitude to improve things for them (and their business). To be successful, you have to be in it for the long haul (and within the right platform). This is not a short-term plan to jump from one industry to the other. This is about showcasing your appetite for being perceived as a leading provider of information for your industry. You do not have to be the biggest, you want to be the most significant.

Share the same core beliefs: it may be based on making a working process easier, it may be making a community a better place; we engage with people who share our beliefs. A relationship may be fundamentally flawed if there is no collaboration. Sharing and speaking about your beliefs will mean you can connect with an audience which will want to stay with you because you can tell a compelling story.

Embrace the belief that you are not an expert, you are a valuable resource with which others can converge. The audience you build is based on the content that you share and the mindset that you shape. The only way to turn initial attraction into a long-term, committed relationship is by showing your audience that you have all the traits that they have been looking for and are 'the one' for them.

OPINION

THE CONTENT VIEW FROM MARKETING INFLUENCERS

If you can open up a dialogue with others, it can provide a wealth of knowledge to share. When you recognize there are people who have a reciprocal sharing mentality, it can become a powerful learning tool.

If you are committed to a cause and others can see that you stand for something, the benefit of sharing knowledge with your audience can become a valuable industry differentiator. Others will be happy to help you if you remain in a state of constant commitment and have the ability to share a message.

If you can show to others proof that you are devoted to your industry, rather than simply stating that you are a trusted resource to work with, your credentials build. This is a long-term investment, rather than a campaign-based mentality. The result is advocacy from a growing audience, which becomes familiar with the way that you cooperate with others.

The *Talking Content Marketing* series of interviews has been an ongoing project since November 2013 within the ID Group website (www.theidgroup.co.uk). The programme is based on interviews with authors, influencers, and luminaries from within the marketing industry.

Each participant is asked six questions within their field of expertise, allowed a week to respond, and the answers are then published on the website. This has provided access to a wealth of knowledge and material. It has also helped shape who I am and has played a significant role in the writing of this book.

Links I would never have thought possible have been created with well-respected people. There was a time when, if we wanted to reach out to an author who had challenged our thinking, a direct conversation was limited via a publisher and we relied on the hope that a letter or email would make its way through. The ability to build a conversation on social channels and to bring it to the spaces that you control, from your email and then to your own website, is one of the greatest assets available to us as individuals and businesses this decade. Technology means that we can now connect across the globe and we can bring the influencers into our offices and living rooms.

Collaborating with others and creating a learning resource for my audience has provided a host of viewpoints and opinion that is regularly available. Plus, people work better when they can share and discuss ideas from a source they find valuable.

Here is a selection of questions and responses from the world's most well-respected marketers. This brings the book to a fitting close by letting the views of others share how the marketing discipline has made a seismic shift.

It would be great for you to join the conversation at the *Talking Content Marketing* interviews on the website and use them as a form of study for the content marketing discipline.

DEFINITION

WHAT DOES CONTENT MARKETING MEAN TO YOU?

For me, good content marketing is simply marketing that people love. Content marketing is a world away from the kind of intrusive, self-interested, pushy marketing that is switching people off in droves. Content marketing means sharing the type of information that customers value and act upon. It's marketing that people in business are proud to create and share.

The word 'content' still causes confusion. In the days before the web, the word was not used in the way it is now, but today it is central to our online world. Content is an integral aspect of today's buying process, and content can be anything at all. A boring video, a dull blog, a terrible Slideshare – they are all content. That's why we differentiate, and say if you want content marketing to work you need valuable content – information that answers your exact question, makes you think, makes you laugh, inspires you, or teaches you something new. Valuable content is content that really hits the spot.

To me, content marketing is the best way of communicating the 'why' of what you do, of finding and delighting your audience, and of winning more of the business you really want.

The right content matters. Here is a simple example. I was looking for a personal trainer recently and picked up two business cards from my gym. I went straight to their websites. The first trainer was no doubt an excellent runner. The website's emphasis is on her running achievements. The second trainer's website was based around a blog – he answered all the questions that I had, for example how do you fit exercise around a busy working day. I trusted he could help me. I chose the trainer with the website that answered MY questions and sounded like he cared – the trainer with a website full of what we call 'valuable content'.

As Mark explains in this book, your job is to provide the right type of information for your particular audience so they know, like, and trust you, and remember you when the time comes to buy. If you get it right, you will win more business. But its benefits go wider still – a fan base which is happy to do your marketing for you, a company aligned – and a happier business. What's not to love about that?

Sonja Jefferson, Co-author of *Valuable Content Marketing*

CULTURAL CHANGE

WHAT IS THE KEY TRIGGER FOR BUSINESSES TO BUY INTO A CONTENT MINDSET?

I am often asked how to convince internal stakeholders and management to buy into content marketing. It's a matter of continuous education and the ability to show the business impact using content. You need to demonstrate the way your content helps your company's business. Let's use email campaigns as an example: can you show that content clicks from your email campaigns convert leads or increase subscribers? Can you triangulate social media followers' comments with your CRM database to identify potential leads for your sales team? The best way to change your management's mindset is through insights. Show how insights into content marketing can be used to impact your business. It's not an easy thing to do, but it's the best way.

Pam Didner, Author of *Global Content Marketing*

HAVE BUSINESSES BECOME TOO STUCK IN THE WAYS THEY HAVE 'ALWAYS DONE IT', WITHIN CHANNELS TO WHICH THEY HAVE BECOME ACCUSTOMED RATHER THAN CHANGING?

We've heard different iterations of 'No one ever got fired for buying IBM/buying TV/buying Facebook.' It continues to change, but it does not mask the underlying point that hiding behind the tried and tested has always indicated safety and security. This is all changing. Look at Uber, Dropbox, Snapchat, Instagram. Companies that have gone from zero to billion(s) in a handful of years, or in some cases months. And in every case, it represents major destabilization to the status quo and/or incumbents. Or think about Dollar Shave Club and Gillette as another example. There are plenty more.

Bill Bernbach once said, 'Safe advertising is the riskiest advertising of all.' Peter Drucker said, 'To defend the past is far riskier than shaping the future.' As the volatility of the marketplace continues to shake up the rules, norms and best practices of 'business as usual', a continued generational shift in marketing and business leadership will in turn usher in a new wave and way of doing business, building brands and specifically authentic, community-driven experiences.

Joseph Jaffe, Author of four books including
Flip the Funnel and *Z.E.R.O.*

WHAT IS THE BIGGEST CHALLENGE FOR BUSINESSES TO MOVE FROM PRODUCT-DRIVEN MESSAGES TO USEFUL CONTENT CREATION AND GIVE VALUE TO THEIR AUDIENCE?

We will continue to see this emerge as one of the most critical issues in the customer journey today: people want a message that fits their needs; they do not have the time nor the inclination to sift through information that's irrelevant or completely misses their needs. In fact, they may get annoyed if they are presented with enough mass marketing. The challenge for business is to get the right content to the right person on the right platform at the right time. And, just as you say, it should provide value to the audience, rather than being a strictly sales-based message.

It's OK to sell, but you've only earned that right after you've built a relationship with people, and to do so, it requires consistency and trust.

Scott Monty, Executive Vice President of Strategy at SHIFT Communications

ARE BUSINESSES GETTING BETTER AT ADOPTING A CONTENT MARKETING APPROACH?

I actually think marketers are getting better at content marketing. We are all on the same learning curve together, so it's kind of exciting. Yes, there is a lot of 'me too' content marketing out there. But thanks to the trackability of digital marketing, we are all being trained by the data to do things better and better and to follow what works. In the end, it will all settle into the usual bell curve: some great content marketers, some really shitty ones, and a big mass in the middle.

Doug Kessler, Cofounder of Velocity partners, a London-based B2B marketing agency

WHAT ARE THE HUMAN TRAITS BUSINESSES NEED TO GRASP?

To build credibility, keep your commitments, make it easy to do business with you, and help me feel like I belong. I just bought a product that stopped working a week later. I went to the website to get this problem resolved and it took me almost 30 minutes to fix. That's not especially helpful. But if they keep their commitments, life will be even more magical.

Chris Brogan, CEO of Owner Media Group, public speaker, and the *New York Times* bestselling author of eight books.

SHOULD BUSINESSES PROVIDE INFORMATION THAT IS RELEVANT TO OUR AUDIENCES RATHER THAN 'FLAG WAVING' THE MERITS OF A BUSINESS OR PRODUCT?

The way to break through in today's incredibly cluttered communication environment is to be inherently useful: to create marketing so valuable that people would pay for it, if you asked them to do so. It is relatively easy to do a one-off Youtility project under the radar. It is something else entirely to embrace useful marketing as a core marketing premise, because doing so requires you to admit that the interruption marketing you've been using for 50 years is not as effective as it once was.

Jay Baer, Author of *New York Times* bestseller Youtility and president of Convince & Convert

IS EGO AND SELF-PROMOTION THE BIGGEST OBSTACLE TO OVERCOME?

Many marketers and sales people steeped in the tradition of product advertising naturally feel drawn to prattle on and on about their products and services. But I have news for you: nobody cares about your products and services (*except you*). Yes, you read that right. What people do care about are themselves and how you can solve their problems. People also like to be entertained and to share in something remarkable. To have people talk about you and your ideas, you must resist the urge to hype your products and services. Instead, create something interesting that will be talked about online. When you get people talking on the web, people will line up to learn more and to buy what you have to offer.

David Meerman Scott, Marketing strategist and bestselling author
of ten books including *The New Rules of Marketing and PR*

STRATEGY

DO WE NEED TO BECOME MORE FOCUSED ON UNDERSTANDING WHO WE ARE, WHAT WE STAND FOR, AND THE AUDIENCE PERSONA, RATHER THAN BECOMING THE SAME AS THE MAJORITY OF THE COMPETITION?

The answer is an unequivocal YES!

The majority of marketers do not have a documented strategy. This is why a campaign mindset still reigns supreme. It's hard to look beyond 'three *touches and a sales call*' without a strategy.

But here is the problem. Buyers are waiting longer to engage with sellers. This means the weight has moved onto marketing's shoulders to create engagement for a longer period of time. And it also means we, as marketers, need to enable sales to get into conversations earlier. Without a strategy, once again, this is not going to happen – not consistently in a way that turns forecasts into reality.

Positioning is critical in a world increasingly filled with crappy content. To rise above the noise, companies need to identify their distinct value and weave that into their communications. Distinct value is the intersection of company strengths with customer needs. It's a pivotal point of distinction that helps increase the relevance of digital marketing strategies – actually all marketing strategies.

The only way to identify distinct value is through intimate knowledge of our audiences – the kind of knowledge facilitated through well-architected audience personas. A content strategy based on products will not get you there. You must know what your buyers, customers, influencers, and end users want, need, and will embrace change to accomplish – as well as why.

Based on those factors, you must understand how your company's story will resonate and design a strategy that incorporates the two perspectives. This level of insight is what's needed to arrive at a distinct value that drives such a high level of relevance that your audiences are compelled to engage with you and buy from you rather than choosing an alternative.

Ardath Albee, CEO and B2B Marketing Strategist, Marketing Interactions, Inc. Author of *Digital Relevance: Marketing Content and Strategies that Drive Results*.

IS A CHANGE OF MINDSET MORE IMPORTANT THAN A CHANGE OF DIRECTION?

I think the first eventually begets the second. Once you embrace content and story as a cornerstone of your marketing – not as a one-and-done campaign, but as a commitment – you cannot help but set the necessary processes and plans in place to plan for the long-term craft and distribution of (and customer engagement with) that content. In other words, you become a media company.

That's not an easy transition to make, I know. But here is the truth: we are already media companies. The question is: how well are you using that access and power?

Ann Handley, Bestselling author of *Everybody Writes* and coauthor of *Content Rules*, Chief Content Officer of MarketingProfs

WHEN EMBRACING A CONTENT MINDSET, DO WE NEED TO APPROACH WITH AUTHORITY AND WARMTH? RATHER THAN FOCUSING ON SEARCH ENGINES, DO WE NEED TO BECOME MORE HUMAN?

Social media is powered by billions of social interactions: millions of tweets with @replies and #hashtags, Facebook posts, comments, Likes and notes, YouTube annotations and replies, Reddit threads, and even 'thumbs-up' on StumbleUpon.

Here is the rub: a social interaction is 'an interpersonal relationship between two or more people that may range from fleeting to enduring'.

See that? It says 'two or more people'. A social interaction, by definition, cannot occur between an inanimate object, an anthropomorphized brand, or even a personified logo. This means all those tweets from your branded tweet stream – they do not matter – they are inauthentic. Those posts are fake and forced attempts at social interaction. They are a prime example of traditional marketers attempting to feign authenticity in an environment powered by authentic personal interactions. Here is a hint: social media is powered by people, not logos.

Here is the good news: you do not need a high-priced ad agency or brand consultant to help you develop your brand's voice. In fact, your 'brand voice' is the sum of the individual voices that make up your company's employee roster. It's the voices of the people who power your vendors and of the customers who buy your products. In today's online universe, everyone has an audience and every individual has a voice. You no longer have to inauthentically personify your brand; your team does this for you.

So, I believe that the future of all branding is personal. Focusing on search engines will not help.

Andrew Davis, Author of *Brandscaping: Unleashing the Power of Partnerships*

DELIVERY

WHY DO YOU THINK STORYTELLING HAS GROWN IN PRECEDENCE AS A BUSINESS COMMUNICATION TOOL OVER THE PAST FEW YEARS?

The rise and popularity of social media sites have ushered in a new era in favour of storytelling. There are more social media channels than ever before and just like consumers, companies are embracing these platforms to share stories related to their products, services, values, corporate culture, events, and more on a daily basis.

The key differentiator among social media sites over the past few years has been the rise of mobile and visual/video content. In the past, text may have reigned supreme, but now photos, videos, infographics, presentations, and more are being used by companies to tell stories as a complement to their marketing and communications efforts.

Jessica Gioglio, Coauthor of *The Power of Visual Storytelling*

COMPANIES BELIEVE THEY DO NOT HAVE A STORY TO TELL, JUST PRODUCTS TO SELL. DO ALL BRANDS HAVE A STORY?

Every single company, no matter how small or large, has a story to tell. A story about its birth, a story about its evolution, a story about its inventions, a story about its passions (yes, every company has a passion: technology, kids, earth, the list goes on), a story about its inventions, a story about its employees and their individual stories. But the biggest story is the story of its mission, its purpose, the 'why' of its existence. That ties back to the passion that started it all, the passion that drove the company's founders and sparked their own journey.

Ekaterina Walter, Author of the *Wall Street Journal* bestseller *Think Like Zuck*, coauthor of *The Power of Visual Storytelling*

ARE BUSINESSES EMBRACING AN ATTITUDE OF BECOMING CREATIVE STORYTELLERS OR MORE FOCUSED ON DISTRIBUTING CONTENT?

Most are clueless. Sorry to be blunt, but that is how I feel. Too often, businesses focus on tactics first. They worry how they are going to get likes and shares and spend little to no time crafting a strategic story that makes sense for them. They see what others do and then try to mimic them. Whatever the latest new tool or viral video is, they want to use it even if it makes no sense.

Every day I hear something along the lines of, '*Well, we make/do _____ so we have no story to tell*', and I always shake my head and laugh. Everyone has a story to tell and, yes, some are harder to find than others, but they are there. That is why you need someone who not only understands the current online world but also has the skills to find and craft your story.

C.C. Chapman, Founder of Never Enough Days and author of *Amazing Things Will Happen*

OPERATIONAL

HOW IMPORTANT IS IT TO BE SEEN AS INFLUENTIAL?

In a crowded marketplace, especially if you operate in a space where knowledge and expertise is your stock in trade and therefore a key differentiator between people and brands, then it's incredibly important.

I like to refer to the word 'authority' – being seen as an authority in your particular niche is critical because an authority is someone people take notice of, listen to – they read their stuff, share their content, and refer them to colleagues and peers; an authority is someone the media will come to for quotes and interviews.

There is nothing wrong with being an expert, by the way, but there are potentially hundreds and thousands of them in any given field whereas there are not as many authorities because – well, let's face it – it takes considerable time and effort to reach that higher level of profile, trust, and respect in the marketplace.

Trevor Young, Author of *microDOMINATION*
and founder of Authority Partners

HAS THE WORLD EXPLODED WITH TOO MANY SELF-PROCLAIMED 'EXPERTS'?

Rule one: a person does not get to declare himself or herself an expert or 'guru' or thought leader. True leaders in the industry demonstrate their expertise through the quality of their actions and insights. Your clientele or audience will choose whether to anoint expert or thought leader status upon you based on those actions.

Usually, if someone calls him or herself a thought leader or guru, it's a signal to me that they are not, no matter how much they'd like to be.

I'm also nervous about the 'expert' tag because the technology changes so rapidly. I once wrote that social media marketing is like trying to eat soup with a fork. You can never control it completely and will always end up with some of your lunch down your shirt because it moves so quickly. And that goes for many areas of marketing today.

So, true experts recognize that they are always learning and experimenting, trying to find a 'better way'. More importantly, true experts are always willing to admit when they do not know or are unsure. 'I do not know' is not an admission of failure. It is recognizing the limits of their expertise. And no one can be a true expert without recognizing his or her own limitations.

Jonathan Crossfield, Storyteller, writer, and content marketing consultant

YOU'VE HIGHLIGHTED YOUR DISCOMFORT WITH THE WORD 'MARKETING' AND REAL FOCUS ON 'MEDIA'. IS THIS THE NEW MINDSET FOR BUSINESSES TO DIFFERENTIATE?

You know, I believe so. We live in a world of undifferentiated products and services. Anything can be manufactured in China, any service or business model replicated. And even when we think we have a winning difference in a feature, studies show that your prospects do not see the difference.

So how do we stand out? How do we provide an experience that's unique? It's in the marketing that we do, which in the realm of content means the media we produce. And that's why every business needs to embrace its own human perspective and unique positioning. You're never going to appeal to everyone, so do not try. But if you appeal strongly to some who happily spread the word, you will be way ahead of your competition.

Brian Clark, Founder and CEO of Copyblogger Media

TACTICS

IS SUCCESSFUL BLOGGING NOT ABOUT TREATING EVERYONE AS A MASS AUDIENCE, BUT INVESTING IN A NICHE AUDIENCE WHO FINDS INTEREST IN WHAT YOU STAND FOR?

If success is about branding and awareness, then sure, it's important that readers like you and what you have to say. Blogging can be a great platform for attracting likeminded thinkers. However, too much of that sameness can breed a lot of boring content. To stand out, blogs in competitive markets need to be more sophisticated to reach the multiple objectives that are possible.

It's entirely reasonable to achieve a mix of goals through blogging using a layered editorial approach. Not everyone reads every post and different people discover blog content through different channels, especially influencers that they follow. So, it's important not to think of your readership as just one customer group. Creating a matrix of audience targets in a blog content plan allows marketers to reach niche vertical audiences by segments like industry as well as the media and influencers that they follow.

Lee Odden, Author of *Optimize* and CEO
of TopRank Online Marketing

DO COMPANIES NEED TO STOP THINKING THAT THEY NEED TO BE SEEN ON ALL CHANNELS AND INSTEAD FOCUS ON QUALITY CONTENT AND ON FEWER CHANNELS?

We've all done it. We think all these channels are opportunities, so we need to be there. Yet we do not have the resources to do it properly, so we fall back to the lowest minimal effort possible of just reposting the same content across the same social channels all the time.

If you're still using a social channel as a one-way megaphone promoting your own content, well, good luck with that.

Yes, it's an efficient process, but you will disappear into the background noise. You're basically just shouting into the wind if all you're doing is using it to tell the world how awesome you are. No one cares. But if you focus on the one or two platforms that are key to your audience, and actually think about the audience with your approach, then an extra 50% of effort per single platform will get you 10 times greater impact.

Todd Wheatland, Author, speaker, and host of The Pivot:
Marketing Backstories podcast

HAS THE ROLE OF TECHNOLOGY AND THE DEMOCRATIZATION OF TRADITIONAL MEDIA - THAT WE CAN NOW BECOME MEDIA COMPANIES - THE GREATEST OPPORTUNITY TO BUILD OUR MESSAGE AND AUDIENCE?

It's by far and away the biggest opportunity to connect with our audience and solidify the brand audience relationship.

A question I always ask a new client, or within a workshop, is 'Google has just closed down Adwords, what are you going to do?' It's a real conversation starter! How do you plug that gap in traffic? The focus is always placed upon that first month. I want businesses to think about the answer long term. So, you're spending £50k a month on Adwords, and that one month of breathing time is enough to devise a strategy to build out your content strategy. Look to months two and three to implement your plan and now there is £150k in the kitty. There is a content team and further time to ensure buy-in across the organization.

That's why I talk (a lot) about breaking convention. For the moment, Adwords will not shut down, but I like businesses to begin thinking about the gradual transition that they could be putting in place. To think about building their brand outside of the conventional marketing world. To build a content-driven brand more meaningful, more purposeful, more memorable. A little more 'you' and a little less ordinary.

Ian Rhodes, Marketing Strategist, Brand Less Ordinary

OUTCOME

WHEN A COMPANY GETS A CONTENT STRATEGY RIGHT, WHAT ARE THE REWARDS?

The rewards I have seen are numerous. The right content strategy unites and empowers all of a business' communications of all sorts across all channels. That includes everything from TV spots to YouTube films, from tweets to lengthy white papers, from print ads to feature documentaries.

The right content strategy also means the business owns the attention of its audience and no longer needs to put as much money into paid media as previously. And the longest-lasting, most valuable reward is that the business' supporters and fans share the content with their friends and colleagues and that sharing, research has shown, can have nine times the reach of traditional messaging and two to four times the impact on purchase behaviour. But to reap those rewards, a business has to understand that content strategy underlies all strategy in a digital-first world where only genuinely valuable content gets any attention.

Kirk Cheyfitz, Co-CEO Story Worldwide

ACKNOWLEGDMENTS

A lot of this book has been achieved by asking others what shapes their perspectives and opinion. To all those who have given me their time, I genuinely appreciate it. Thank you to those who let me delve deeper and provided their contributions within this book, especially Robert Rose for the foreword.

I would also like to thank the support of David Woods from LID Publishing who let me bring an idea to fruition and take a publishing route that has proved to be a rewarding experience. To the LID team who have also supported the Once Upon A Time project, huge thanks.

Finally, thanks to those who have helped me learn. From the company that went into liquidation and owed me a lot of money, to the people who asked me to pitch for work only to give the business to someone else, you have helped me grow. I understand that every obstacle becomes a motivator to shape who we are and the businesses we represent. The recession has claimed many businesses, but to those who have ridden the wave and still here, there is a story to tell and lessons that have been learned.

Sometimes it's the journey we make that is more enriching than the final destination...

22

years

building on our success

- 1993 Madrid
- 2007 Barcelona
- 2008 Mexico DF & Monterrey
- 2010 London
- 2011 New York & Buenos Aires
- 2012 Bogota
- 2014 Shanghai & San Francisco